ROGER WHITE

ANOTHER SONG, ANOTHER SEASON

ANOTHER SONG
ANOTHER SEASON

POEMS AND PORTRAYALS

by

ROGER WHITE

GEORGE RONALD
OXFORD

First published by
George Ronald
46 High Street, Kidlington, Oxford OX5 2DN

0-85398-087-X (cased)
0-85398-088-8 (paper)

Acknowledgements

The following poems appeared in *The Bahá'í World* and are re-
printed by permission of the Universal House of Justice: *New
Song*, vol. XIV, © 1974; *Glimpses of 'Abdu'l-Bahá* and *Lines
from a Battlefield*, vol. XV, © 1975; *A Metropolis of Owls, The
Pioneer* and *Suppliant: Bahjí*, vol. XVI, © 1978.

Mr White's 'Mark Tobey: A Letter and Two Snapshots' first
appeared in *World Order*, vol. 12, no. 2, Spring 1978, pp. 34–6.
Copyright © 1978 by the National Spiritual Assembly of the
Bahá'ís of the United States of America.

PRINTED IN THE UNITED STATES OF AMERICA

To Kathleen and John White
who called me forth
and set me on this journey

CONTENTS

vii

FOREWORD

Another Song, Another Season is the first selection of Roger White's poetry to be published in book form, although single poems have appeared before. The selection has been made with a view to maintaining homogeneity, a difficult task when confronted with the prolific and wide-ranging promptings of his muse.

The frequently observed dichotomy in individuals between outward circumstance and inner spiritual truth is a valid poetical subject; these poems, notably the 'Portrayals', go beyond exemplifying the fact and disclose the reality of unity in diversity. The unifying spirit is the response of widely varied individuals to the Revelation of Bahá'u'lláh. The portraits are of real people, heroes and martyrs and servants of the Bahá'í Faith, many of them our contemporaries, which increases our interest a thousandfold. Keith, 'a looker', but 'brainy' too; Martha, dowdy and unimpressive outwardly, but able to set aflame the hearts of men with that divine love which consumed her; Fred Mortensen, the dropout boy who hoboed his way to see the Master and achieved eternal fame. The theme fascinates our poet.

He has the remarkable gift of knowing how to present high themes—nobility, dedication, the beauty of sacrifice, the eternal battle of the soul—in modes of common speech and everyday concepts, an ability rooted in his revulsion to the meretricious, the sanctimonious and the pi. His poetry is spiritual and religious but neither didactic nor obscure.

The inclusion of a few poems in lighter vein is felicitous, for it leads us to hope that in further volumes his predilection for shying tomatoes at top hats will be indulged—to our delight and his.

Haifa   *David Hofman*
1978

PART ONE: PORTRAYALS

O ye apostles of Bahá'u'lláh! . . . Behold the portals which Bahá'u'lláh hath opened before you! Consider how exalted and lofty is the station you are destined to attain; how unique the favours with which you have been endowed. . . . I fervently hope that in the near future the whole earth may be stirred and shaken by the results of your achievements. . . . Be not concerned with the smallness of your numbers, neither be oppressed by the multitude of an unbelieving world . . . Exert yourselves; your mission is unspeakably glorious.

'Abdu'l-Bahá

MARTHA ROOT
1872–1939

A dowdy girl, was Martha, and a real gadabout . . .
(remark by a contemporary)

Have patience, Martha,
we shall forget
the hastily-hemmed hand-me-downs
the laddered hose
the horrent hair
shall understand you yet,
cease to care
whether virtue be photogenic, dare
see in your eye's lens
the apocalyptic images ineffaceably etched there—
the poisoned air
the towers afire
the maimed trees
the human pyre—these
which sent you hurtling in exquisite arc
across the blackening sky,
your life a solitary warning cry
against engulfing dark
and ultimate night.
Your eyes were dippers
used against the fire,
purchased brief respite
that on the ramparts might arise
the legioned guardians of light.

Be patient:
we may yet ourselves become
God's gadabouts,
meteoric, expire
Martha-like,
in conflagrant holy urgency.

3

A LETTER TO KEITH

Now Keith, she was a 'looker' ...

(remark by a contemporary)

Why did you do it, Keith,
And you a looker?
Not your usual religious dame
in need of a good dentist
and a fitted bra.
Not one of those skinny ones
who make it their painful duty to love mankind
and purse their lips a lot
to let you know it isn't easy.
Not one of those.
Sharp dresser, too.
And brainy.
Not every man's kind of woman
but a looker.
And a real good talker, too.
It makes no sense, Keith.
You could have put your passion to another use.

We grow them odd here in Michigan,
but you were an odd one even for us—
why, just your name, for starters.
And all your mooning about the library,
reading too much,
making notes in little books. And your preaching.
I suppose your life was full enough
but your interest in God—was that normal?
We always said you could pray the paint off a barn door
at twenty paces, but we meant no harm.
It was as though you were always looking for something
you hadn't found.

And gallivanting around the world like you did,
visiting the Maoris and savages like that,
which we had only ever seen in *National Geographic*.
In those days we thought we were doing pretty good
if we made a trip to Chicago.
Nobody faulted you for going to the Holy Land,
you always were the studious kind
and they've got a helluva lot of religion there.

We heard you were sent on a special mission
to fight for a good cause.
Well, you'd be just the girl for that;
but why Persia, Keith?
Life still isn't worth a nickel there
and what do they know about plumbing?
With a tongue like yours, I'll bet you told
those folks a thing or two.
And when word got back that you had died
there's some as said
you'd found what you wanted at last.
I'm one who thinks you did, Keith,
who thinks you did.

All these years later
standing at the marker they put up for you here at home
and reading those words
and listening to what these decent people are saying
about you being a glorious martyr and all—
I'm bawling,
me a grown man,
three sons and wife in the grave
and not what you'd call sentimental.

Why did you do it, Keith,
and you a looker?

LOUIS G. GREGORY

1874–1951

He is like pure gold; that is why he is acceptable in any market, and is current in every country.

'Abdu'l-Bahá

Across the angry decades that
separate us from him
may there still be found
true and stainless words
unwarped by the suppositions
and suspicions of these hurtful times
to honour this gentleman of colour?

We need the lesson of this life;
need know that the alchemy
of service and obedience
mints coin of purest gold.
In his modesty he almost eludes us
but we will know him yet.

Travel, the Master said,
*I want them to see you;
you are very dear to me.*

And dear to us, Louis,
who see you now
and love, as He,
O Louis, love,
even as the beauty of your dusk,
your gleam.

VISIT TO A VETERAN

*I often thought that Horace Holley might have been a bit of a
rake when he was young, but he straightened up real good.*

(remark by a contemporary)

Wilmette, 1953

You had a mandarin's tranquillity,
A Jesuitical poise, but I was keen to see
If the legends of you held validity.
You knew, of course, but smiled and offered tea.

'The ego our sole, our deadliest foe . . .'
I nibbled cake and mused it might be so.
'This battle is the bravest act I know . . .'
I feigned agreement and arose to go.

Homage to homily! Cliché well spun!
A wasted meeting—and this our only one—
The gift then not seen (my struggle scarce begun)
Your face: archive of victory sorely won.

'ABDU'L-GHAFFÁR OF IṢFAHÁN

What fish is this that struggles to the shore,
For whom this absence is a fiery death,
And, plunging, finds but anguish all the more,
Each scorching wave a torment to his breath?

What lure aland inspires this frantic flight?
Toward whose strong skein turns he his questing eye?
The poet told this knowing fish's plight:
Here sea; here hapless, burning lover, dry.

7

MASTER CRIMINAL

*From every land Thou hearest the lamentations
of them that love Thee, and from every direc-
tion Thou hearkenest unto the cries of such as
have recognized Thy sovereignty. . . . Thou
knowest full well, O my God, that their only
crime is to have loved Thee.*

Bahá'u'lláh

Tell, Duarte Vieira, kindly tell,
What crime won you a prison cell?

Your testament, a biscuit tin—
What, Duarte Vieira, was your sin?

What was the error of your ways
That heaven's Concourse sings your praise?

What offence did you commit?
Tell, that we may follow it.

Reveal your secret so that we
May, too, gain immortality.

Our skulking fears by you allayed,
We seek a crime so richly paid.

All Africa now vastly blessed:
Bahá's felon laid to rest.

Tell, Duarte Vieira, kindly tell,
What crime won you a prison cell?

MARION JACK

1866–1954

Let them remember Marion Jack . . .
                                        Shoghi Effendi

We are not menaced by this one
in our silent, steely rise to power.
The unseen worm
sleeps blissfully
in the silver apple.

This is not a master.
The world justifiably ignores
the conventional inept daubs
and we affirm
that charitable neglect.
Our hand will not tremble
as we reach for our brush;
no standard born of her
rebukes our palette.

Not even as a woman
does she intimidate.
The body is a commonplace,
the domestic bulk foreshadowing
varicose veins. We see her
as a cardiac. The face,
an artifact, looks homemade.
If our glance lingers
it is to find confirmation
that fat people are jovial.
Observe the open grin
that cannot imagine
rejection or destruction.

Let us pass her by,
one of those useless people
drowsing on park benches
who would embarrass our friends.
We need not dignify her paintings
by affording them critiques;
history in its mercy
will dispose of them.
We deal in success,
we understand these things.

But what is this achievement
looming indestructibly
from the acme of another arc?

> *Mourn loss immortal heroine . . . greatly*
> *loved and deeply admired by 'Abdu'l-Bahá*
> *shining example pioneers present future*
> *generations East West . . .*

The worm stirs.
Precipitately
the apple tumbles forward.
Holding it in the mind's blue light
the teeth engage—
but this shall taste of ashes.

> *Envie not greatnesse . . .*
> *Be not thine own worm*

How chill the murk
behind our opaque, earthbound eyes.
Regard the larger canvas: a masterwork.

> *Marion! Guide us as we seize the brush!*
> *Teach us the colours of immortality!*

EAGLE

Lua Getsinger
1871–1916

Mother-teacher of the American Bahá'í Community . . .

Shoghi Effendi

Studio of Juliet Thompson
New York
13 June 1912

I

Here at the giddy summit
of our acute and secret need,
above desire's burning desert
and ambition's treacherous bog,
in this perch gained painfully
by the heart's frail ladder
and reason's faulty bridge—
all means by which we sought approach—
we nestle in the dappling light
in His love's green and leafy warmth.

We who think we know Him,
who found in Him
more than we could have known to want
of the Good of goodness,
who see Him as Father,
our Christ-need dream fleshed out
and fruit of every crèche made real,
Son of the Eternal Sun,
Perfection wrought ideal,
whitest white of White,
the rosest Rose,

11

prismatic fire of diamond,
honey's amber inmost essence
and flower's unseen core—
now are given more.

> *I am the Centre of God's Covenant,*
> He said.

Despite our pain and vertigo
the goal not gained!
Our understanding sags and sighs
beneath the blue and reeling loft
we must claim else die
on this flint and lonely precipice.

If eagle will know sky
it must trenchantly seize air
in plumate frenzy,
pummel,
conquer,
rise,
soar—
be eagle.

> *You must understand this: I am the*
> *Centre of the Covenant in your midst.*

In the throbbing hiatus
as we mutely cower
He reads one heart:

> *Lua, I appoint you the Herald of the*
> *Covenant.*

In tears the fledgeling lunges
toward a chaste and unknown splendour:
'O Master, re-create me for this task!'

We see her earthfree
in avian ascent
sweep toward heaven's arch;
her receding joyous cries
flake down
faint as echo's echo.

We would have this azure authority,
ask strengthening,
wing and tendon,
for this flight.

THE PURCHASE
Ḥájí Ja'far-i-Tabrízí

Afflictive woe unbearable; they grieve.
One uncalm mourner cannot reconcile to this
And through unreasoned act buys their reprieve,
Below his drooped mouth carves a scarlet grin of bliss.
Egregious deed attended by reward,
He lives and, exiled, gains reunion with his Lord.

If madness purchase immortality
Grant compounded madness, love's full insanity

HOW TO SUCCESSFULLY
CONDUCT THE ROBBERY OF
A LITTLE OLD LADY

*Toward the end of her life, while serving as a Bahá'í pioneer
in the Canary Islands, Prudence George (1896–1974) of
the British Bahá'í community had her handbag snatched
by a young thief. Upon her calling aloud the Greatest
Name the boy dropped the purse and fled in confusion.
Prudence was left calling him back in order to listen to the
Message of Bahá'u'lláh.*

I am the first to admit that
William Carlos Williams is the ultimate authority
on how to conduct a funeral
but I'm glad you came to me about this matter.

Mine was the perfect crime, you see,
I retired wealthy at an early age
and my victim and I have become the best of friends.
We sometimes sit around of an evening
and reminisce about the robbery.
What could be nicer, more civilized?
I'm able to say with some little pride
that I'm something of an expert in my field.
Williams couldn't help you here;
you did well to come to me.

I'm afraid you handled your little affair
rather poorly, my dear chap.
Admittedly you chose your victim well.
She was an obvious mark, of course,
conspicuously a foreigner
moving through the town with the
curious innocence and vulnerability
of the stranger.
Her age was in your favour—
older ladies can rarely run very fast.

You never know about their lung power, of course.
Some seem to have waited all their lives
for a chance to indulge in some
justified high-decibel screaming—
but that's a chance you take.

Yes, she seemed a good choice,
as victims go, but you bungled it, young fellow.
There was little excuse for it—
you slim as a jack-knife,
capable of moving fleetly and with stealth—
not that these were necessary qualifications
for the job.

No, it was your mistaken judgement.
That's how you muffed it, my boy,
in going after the handbag.
No value there.
If you'd given her half a chance
she'd have offered you a pearl beyond price.
If you'd handled it correctly
it would have been a piece of cake
as we used to say in the trade.

Now next time, my lad, here's what you do.
Forget about handbags—they're usually filled
with bus tokens, hairpins,
photographs of grandchildren,
throat lozenges, theatre programmes,
shopping lists, shredding facial tissues,
grubby pencil stubs and astonishing quantities of lint—
rarely the sleek travellers' cheques
you imagine sprout there.

So forget the purse.
Instead, approach the victim eagerly
wearing a friendly smile.

15

Extend your hand in a warm greeting
and say: Madam, have you anything to tell me?
And the pearl is yours!
There, you see, as easy as taking
candy from a baby.
Duck soup, as it were.

For heaven's sake, lad,
take a little pride in your work.

Go now,
I think you are ready.

THE DANCER

Catherine Rudyerd (Heward) Huxtable

Knight of Bahá'u'lláh (Gulf Islands, Canada)
1932–1967

This frailest, seated girl who'd choose to dance,
Yet cheats ungracious nature's cumbering trial,
Gallops her mount without a backward glance,
Knows well she will be with us but a while
And undeterred by body's withering blight
Achieves the valorous victory of a Knight.

Wariest bird, the shadow ever near,
Outpours her song—we would not have it end—
Lavishes joy, nor deigns to squander tears,
So imminent reunion with the Friend.
Departing then, example left as trust,
To Africa consigns her fragrant dust.

She dances now, enthroned in love's fair keep.
We see her vacant chair and do not weep.

FUJITA WITH PILGRIMS

Dearly loved tireless steadfast Saichiro Fujita ...His rank in van-guard first Japanese believers his labours World Centre his dedication humility sincerity love will for ever be remembered ...

The Universal House of Justice
(Cablegram of 7 May 1976)

I

What was 'Abdu'l-Bahá really like?
      The Master was always very kind to me.
But what did you hear Him say?
      Everything He wanted to teach us is
      in His Writings and His example.
To think you had the bounty of serving Him!
      I never felt that I could do very much for
      'Abdu'l-Bahá. One thing I did was
      perhaps acceptable—
      sometimes I made Him laugh.
And what did He say to you?
      He told me to be a good boy.

II

There is a rightness in our meeting here.
He is proprietorial in the garden,
the dwarfing verdure seems to nuzzle him.
Acquitted of triviality by a pain and loneliness
that might instruct us,
rescued a halo's-breadth from isolating sainthood
by an exonerating intolerance and his need for us
but still a holy man
he accepts our homage not in full innocence
yet more in his Master's right than his own,
mikado of mirth,
the Servant's servant.

Impaled upon our need for validation,
(Approve us, you by Him approved!)
above our pity or patronage,
with a rare awareness of his assured immortality,
he offers for our Polaroid delight a harlequinade,
inattentive to the dignity he has unassailably achieved.
Against our expectation of dogmatic declamation
or prescription for joy
his pantomimed haiku attests: There is no mystery here;
                    only fidelity and service.
The children accept the sage as secretless,
admit him to their world,
converse in a language we have lost.
We chafe at the edge of their enchantment.
We are aspiring esoterics,
giddy with statistics and formulae,
swooningly obsessed with apocrypha and eschatology;
our questions swarm through the mute garden
like raucous insects.
Sedated by sunlight
the geranium gape in crimson consternation.
His certitude is chivalrous, does not accuse;
it is older than the garden.

III

Our anguish cannot hold him.
Eluding our slender claim
he turns from our doubt to the flowers
and silent concerns,
ambling away with a wink and a wave
betokening our affirmation.
He courts annihilation;
a fairer garden calls.
Beyond our view his comic stance is shed;
he is listener, suppliant, awaiter.
His yearning towers
with the patience and solemnity of trees.

IV

We had not thought the journey such a lonely one.
In the backwash of his inviolate renunciation we stand,
waist-deep in the dumb geranium,
disconsolately tracing our distance from the goal,
churning the weightless air
with our questions and our words,
our endless words.

Someone asks: Did you take his picture?

Haifa
April 1975

A CUP OF TEA

Persian Muslims will tell you often that the Bábís bewitch
or drug their guests so that these, impelled by a fascination
which they cannot resist, become similarly affected with
what the aforesaid Muslims regard as a strange and
incomprehensible madness.

New York, 1912:

No more tea, Emma dear, you have been more than kind and
the cake was most delicious. The strawberries are extraordinary this year, are they not . . . sweet and plump; like small red
hearts.

But returning to your question, yes, I have been seeing dear Miss Thompson and her friends; Juliet is a charming and talented girl and her friends are kindly.Many of them are well placed—somehow one doesn't quite dare hope for that among the religious, if I may say so. I try to warn Miss Thompson to hold little hope for me—as you know, I'm essentially pragmatic—but she does insist so sweetly that sometimes I attend. She is always gracious at the meetings though I understand little of what she says—since her visit to Palestine she has seemed—how shall I say—not quite of this world; she lives in a state of ecstasy. She talks of nothing but the one she calls the Master—an occult-sounding term; I quite dislike it—but I confess he does intrigue me; I mean, a prisoner for forty years and now at an advanced age coming to America teaching a message of brotherly love and peace—it's like a fable. The newspapers are full of it, of course.

Miss Thompson has been beside herself since learning he would come and I naughtily allowed her to persuade me to meet him, not giving her false hope by permitting her to see how avidly curious I was. You can picture it—my pretending indifference yet half fearing she would cease insisting, and then my casting about for some means to accomplish this without upsetting my husband. Wingate is an avowed agnostic, as he eagerly informs anyone who will listen, and no doubt would disown me. His conception of my social role outside the home, I'm afraid, extends no further than my service on the Opera League and my charities; and he has always been embarrassed by what he calls my brother's Episcopalian delusions. Charles studied for the ministry, you know, until he contracted tuberculosis. After he regained his health Wingate rescued him and gave him a place in the business.

But where was I? Oh yes, the Master—how queer that that name should come so readily to my lips; 'Abdu'l-Bahá or 'Abbás Effendi would be proper forms of address, I suppose.

Despite my subterfuge, arranging an appointment was not so easily accomplished; there were many meetings but all were crowded—devotees pouring in from as far away as California, I hear. But at last we succeeded in finding a mutually agreeable time and I was Miss Thompson's guest at a gathering at someone's home—a rather good address—though what Juliet told the hostess I cannot think, and indeed I never met her, so great the crush. A strange assortment—some orientals—Persians, I suppose—a coloured gentleman—Wingate would use another term but, you see, one can in the South without offence—two Chinese, and some of what one might describe as the labouring class; a struggling artist or two, and one who might have been a poet, from Miss Thompson's seemingly endless circle of co-enthusiasts. Others, too, of course, who appeared both charming and distinguished, but on the whole one was struck both by the ordinariness of the people in the group and fascinated by the idea of their being linked together through curiosity or devotion. And the Master was present —'Abdu'l-Bahá—and he appeared—how shall I say—oh, noble, majestic, serene—it was rather as though a great light had entered the room—do you find me sentimental? One felt an overpowering need to win his approval—like a child with an adored teacher. And he spoke. Not at length, but with extreme simplicity and power. His voice is gentle, hypnotic, one might say irresistible. I scarcely remember the words—it was rather his presence which compelled—but something of his father's sufferings and his message, and a few words about his own imprisonment—the words seemed the least part of it. One could not resist feeling a sympathy, of course, but for me what he said was not the central point. How can I say this and be sure I am understood—as he spoke I asked myself: why is he here; what does he want of us; he is not young—what can possibly come of this journey in the West?

And it came to me that his being here represents an unvoiced invitation—perhaps I should say command, for it is his presence which expresses it rather than what he says—a command, then, that we make an adjustment in our lives—am I making sense? I almost exclaimed aloud: 'He wants us to be like him!' Not in an imitative way—not that—but to step into his world, and to somehow transform this one. And I wondered if the others knew this too—perhaps this is what Miss Thompson has been telling me all along and I simply have not understood. But it bore in on me there in his presence—profoundly bore in—that he asks us to make an adjustment of the soul, if I may use that term—to become spiritually renewed.

This all happened in a flash, as these things do, Emma, and there was more. In that moment I knew I might— if I were free—what shall I say—follow him, in the sense Miss Thompson uses that term. Oh, not on my knees in the dust as she doubtless would—though perhaps that too—but, in my own way, follow him; that I might become one of those women who weep at his mention; that he might represent a standard to which one could devote one's life—forgive me if I ramble, but I scarcely know words to describe this and if I embarrass you I'll stop. It's just that there is no one to whom I have been able to tell it all. I'm inhibited in speaking to Miss Thompson—she's so hopeful of my being won over and in fairness I must not encourage her. There I was—in my mind—throwing myself at his feet, sobbing, and covering them with kisses. It was most unsettling.

But in the same moment of realizing this truth about myself I felt a sense of deep loss—a heart-piercing loss. I heard myself saying—not aloud, of course, though I scarcely knew at that time what I might have done—heard myself saying 'It's too late for me!' And tears stung my eyes at that instant. Pictures of Wingate and the children flashed into mind, and a picture of our house and myself presiding at one of Wingate's functions.

And I looked about the room and thought, how can I open my home to all these people? How can I present them to Wingate's mother? In following the Master, you see, you open your door upon the world. My choices have been made, I realized. And in my feeling of loss I saw the faces around me suddenly as alien, hateful—in that moment I felt a loathing even for Miss Thompson who has been the essence of kindness. The people appeared—how shall I put it—smug and conspiratorial, a closed circle. I felt excluded and I detested them. I saw them as Wingate might see them, as pitiable objects of derision—as calf-eyed and fawning, mooning about like biblical figures at the feet of Christ in a shabby tableau. They seemed naïve, even incredibly stupid. Of what use are any of these to him, I thought? He is of a different world! What can possibly come of this journey he is making, these talks, this pathetic handful? How can any of this matter?

All of this in a split second, as I said. And then I closed my eyes against my tears. It is perhaps as well I had not met the hostess because then, unforgivably—I blush to say it—I fainted. The room was stifling and I had unwisely worn a velvet frock. I have never in my life engaged in that deplorable female diversion—Wingate's mother faints at every conceivable opportunity—I despise the practice, always having supposed it to be an artifice. But there it was—picture it, if you can, Emma. I must have blacked out for only a moment—someone was fussing about and making well-meaning but clumsy efforts to loosen my collar, and my eyes opened to see the Master rising and coming towards me bearing the cup of tea someone had just placed in his hand. He came to me urgently—and, yes, tenderly—and handed me his cup. 'Drink! Drink!' he said, and his voice and eyes were almost stern. Wherever he is the Master is the centre of attention so of course all eyes were upon me as I took a timid sip. No offence to you, dear, but never have I tasted such tea as from his hand. And then he smiled dazzlingly and leaning down to me whispered in English—his tone was so pitched that no one heard—'It is acceptable.' His eyes appeared to lend a significance beyond what the words conveyed. And then he turned and the others engaged him. I was happy no longer to be the focal point of the room. Soon it was over and we all left. I have not seen Miss Thompson since, nor answered her calls. And I will not discuss this with her—isn't it strange, but I feel this is private, in some acutely intense way it is mine. Obviously I must extricate myself from her group—gently, of course, for I have no wish to hurt her. However laudable or desirable the objectives of her circle, it is too late for me; perhaps it is even too late for all of us. How my husband and my parents would scorn all my gushing—all the emotional tumult that meeting has unleashed—though perhaps I do not really know them at all, and Wingate least of all. Do you ever feel that those you love are strangers? I cannot imagine how I appear to my own husband and children or explain the sense of remoteness from them I sometimes experience. It is odd to feel divorced from one's own life's centre.

But, anyway, too late, you see, too late. As Wingate says, this is the age of reason and enlightenment, the century of prosperity and progress and peace, and the world struggles along well enough without its seers and sages. He may well be right—he makes a study of these things. But, Emma, the Master! If only you could see him!

Extraordinary, wasn't it, his saying what he did? I wonder whether I shall ever understand it.

MARK TOBEY : A LETTER AND
TWO SNAPSHOTS

It is one thing to paint a picture, and another to experience it.

Mark Tobey

24 April 1976
Haifa

I came along too late to know you well, Mark—
geography and our ages against it, an ocean between—
so, learning of your death, I sift for photographs
and memory serves up only two.
Others must have many; I am content with mine.
Both speak to me of courage: you will not find that strange.

The Temple in Wilmette is background to the first.
It was 1953, in spring. I came,
new to conferences and the House of Worship,
excited, claiming it all, drunk with seizure.
You were on the stairs looking curiously lonely in the
        bubbling crowd.
I saw the wistfulness.
Someone whispered your name and I broke away,
rushing at you in adolescent ebullience,
bristling to possess my first celebrity.
You were a Bahá'í—public—mine—
like the Temple and the nine-pointed star.
I saw your momentary wince,
the flash of what I knew to be
a customary irritability,
saw you as victim, as target, as too often possessed
and made, trivially, an unwilling familiar.
Meetings and martyrs are of many kinds.
In that moment I could have wept for your vulnerability.

What name do we give the process
that translates private pain into human service?
We clutch the ready cliché 'he did the Bahá'í thing'
and hope we're understood.
I do not know what need you read in me
but instantly you took that step,
leaned towards my abashment.
I cannot measure your cost,
saw only the warm smile,
the reaching out, the bestowal of the gift.
You would have me be your fellow-conspirator,
pretended rescuer, playmate for Peck's bad boy.
'Let's escape and have some tea', you said,
and led me away, appointing me your shield,
feigning to be led. The crowd would have held you
but for the perfection of your pantomime:
two established friends
hastening through the jostle
to the deserved privacy of a longstanding, self-promised tryst,
the venerable one acknowledging greetings on the fly,
the younger appearing the more eager to be off.
Do not suggest it was mere expediency—
we know when we are used.

The stratagem succeeded.
Companionably seated in the café, in snug anonymity,
I was dizzy with expectation: what would be revealed?
Soon I knew.
You spoke of the weather in Seattle,
              the food in Switzerland,
              of arthritis,
              of growing old.
And not a word about painting or the Faith.
I was not long puzzled. In that pedestrian flow
I was given access: Mark Tobey was revealed.
You *are* a painter—you *paint:* there, on canvas, your words.

26

You *are* a Bahá'í: befriending the young stranger,
offering tea, presenting the Faith in *transaction*.
Even then I was grateful to be spared discipleship
and a gratuitous verbal tour of those landmarks
that trace the outermost fringes of the stronghold of belief,
or a recital of those polite bywords we erect as barriers
at the remotest courtyard of identity
to discourage rather than invite entry or homecoming.

We separated smoothly; I, your debtor, not made to feel one.
It was as though we had spoken many times
and grown secure in our partings.

More than twenty years have passed; the picture does
       not fade.
I have my own Mark Tobey, unretouched,
and often I consult it when courage is the prize.
I would not trade it and no, Mark, it is not for sale.

           .   .   .

London, 1963: spring again, the Jubilee,
another picture, an even larger crowd.
I did not look for you among the thousands but
found myself seated again at tea with you
in a random gathering,
you winking playful recognition of a long-ago ruse.
When, by chance, we were alone
you spoke of the weather in London,
             the food in France,
             of arthritis
             of growing old,
             of loneliness.
Again I was not puzzled:
By then had seen your paintings, had trembled,
had heard and seen you in the white writing,
knew your themes, your swoon.

27

'Martyrs are not popular subjects', you once remarked.
I did not ask why you painted martyrs, Mark,
though I marveled at your valour.
Martyrs bear witness to belief;
they are the supreme lovers;
they die for love.
Who would paint martyrs in an age that debases the word
to a tag of parlour-game psychology?
Who would dare paint love in a world that has forgotten it?
Who, indeed, would frame and hang his soul?

AND ALL THE ANGELS LAUGHING
Bernard Leach
In Memoriam

7 May 1979

Bernard beckoning shyly at the door.
Mark beaming now
and Reg agog with glee,
and all the angels laughing
welcomingly.
Does Juliet excitedly scatter
the frisky cherubs, pour
equivalent of tea,
maternally attentive to the chatter
of the reunited three—

boyish, how incorrigibly
boyish!—even in their immortality,
speaking delightedly
of palette, glaze and brush,
chuckling companionably,
till Juliet cries 'Hush! One at a time!'
and Mark, the wag,
exclaims 'the tea's *divine*,
dear Bernard, but Juliet's a nag!'
and the air is warm with laughter.

Does this amaze? Would we
ask more of celestial matter,
or know that heaven peopled by such folks
can well accommodate their jokes?
Can love's Kingdom be
less domestic than the glimpses we
are given? Need we strain toward etheriality?
Perhaps. Still, domesticity
even there must have its lot.
God's economy would will
that it's the known good we regain
at first, and His surprises after,
which earth's grief but restrain.
Leave them to their laughter
and discussion of the circle and the dot.
See! Bernard tells an anecdote,
describes a favourite pot.
It is we who speak of pain.

THE APPOINTMENT

In 1907 Corinne True carried to 'Akká a parchment scroll containing the names of more than a thousand American Bahá'ís who asked permission to erect a House of Worship. Hiding it behind her on the divan she first presented the gifts sent by the friends. But the Master strode across, reached behind her and grasped the parchment and held it aloft: 'This is what gives me great joy. Go back and work for the Temple, it is a great work. Devote yourself to this project. Make a beginning, and all will come right.'

Pilgrim notes of Corinne True

Wilmette, Illinois: 1 May 1912

I

There is another kind of clock
its cogwheels fixed
in the unknowable convolutions
of God's mind,
perhaps our galaxies
its smallest jewels,
a clock that marks
some celestial piecing
of eternity,
one that runs silently,
invisibly,
forever,
fluidly forward or back,
cancelling our time,
its tick perpetual,
attuned to the omniscient
and eternal heart.
It is respectful
of the boundaries we erect

against the terror
and the mystery;
humours our pasteboard timepieces;
is charitable to our insolent need
to feel, invulnerably,
that our measures are solid
and docile to our will,
that *real* is *real*
and *then* and *now* stay put
and our world does not slip
or warp or wobble.

II

Coincidence is the
uneasy name
we give stark moments
when intervention
rises up to melt our mathematics
or intersect our schemes.
Our departure inexplicably delayed,
we read of the sunken ship,
the crippled, flaming plane,
with congratulatory satisfaction
and a faint contempt for
others' luck and planning.
The fortuitous arrival
of a letter
we glibly assign to impulse
and hold hope that horoscopes
foretold the sudden meeting
that brought love
there on the ugly, accustomed street
under the stranger's shared parasol
in an unseasonable shower.

III

And so we are waiting
inflexibly correct
under the canvas marquee
for the Master to take His part
in our rehearsed pattern,
faint with excitement,
flush with historicity,
adjusting our impeccable neckties,
fingering our fashionable pearls,
stroking the gold watches
that pulse in the vest pocket
or wilt, pendent on slender chain,
at the bosom,
their claim negated
by another Time.
We long for authority
to check the uncontrollable
lakeborn breeze
that chills the perspiration
beading in our palms.

IV

Enthralled,
loving Him,
we see His radiance approach,
mirror to the sun.
His freely vigorous stride
sets the shining robe
twining and swirling
into eloquent motion.
His head is raised
to drink the wind-fed air.
Unfaithful to our plan

He leaves the carriage,
comes on foot
in perfect grace.
Soundlessly we gasp
at humility and majesty
in peerless balance.

V

*The power which has gathered you
here today notwithstanding the cold
and windy weather is indeed mighty
and wonderful. It is the power of
God, the divine favour of Bahá'u'lláh
which has drawn you together . . .*

Appropriate to our expectations
are His simple words.
Our souls drift
like somnolent fish
in the warm tide of His approval.
We do not strain to understand.
Secure in our ritual
we may not see,
as in His eye,
the Temple risen,
long since risen,
lighted,
a pulsating refuge,
peopled . . .
and beyond that,
and beyond.

VI

He makes a gesture
with the golden trowel,

graciously accepts that emblem-toy
as He does our childlike love—
but service is His Call.
With axe and shovel, then,
the soil is turned,
as unresisting to His hands
as our hearts to His words.
Compliantly the earth parts
before that force;
perhaps we only imagine
that it pulses with expectancy.
Under our heavy hats of felt or feathers
the brows throb:
what seed does He plant here?

VII

The Temple will have a spiritual influence,
a tremendous effect upon civilization.
From this beginning, thousands of Temples
will rise . . .

Again the schedule is sundered.
Beckoned by His smile
the solemn, silent friends
surge towards His upraised hand,
open the earth,
each a spadeful,
in the name of all mankind,
for this Temple shall be Mother.
Our doubt dissolves
in the calm assurance of His words
as we crane toward His vision.

VIII

We had politely grimaced
at the well-known tale

34

of Nettie Tobin's *voices*
instructing her to bring a stone;
we pictured her squat,
bustling, inelegant,
middle-aged and panting,
her red-faced frenzied scuttle,
weaving her course
in shabby, tilting shoes
across uneven ground,
trundling the child's cart
with a splintered rock
rejected by a builder,
her contribution of a cornerstone.
New to love
we smiled indulgently upon her zeal
and did not know our condescension.
'Now all is in readiness', she had said,
as a complacent housewife might remark
surveying her set table,
but wondered, too, at her impulsion
as she stood alone
at the bleak and vacant site.

IX

And now His hands are on the stone.
He turns to it
as to an expected guest,
His eyes caressing the jagged shape
as they would
a dear friend's face,
this appointment
longingly awaited.
He gently nestles the rock to rest
in the raw brown loam
where we yearn to take its place
and earn the light smile that

plays across His face.
He turns and speaks:

The Temple is already built!

X

We almost understand.
'What a wonderful lesson!
How kind and utterly sweet He is!' we say,
glancing at our watches,
gathering up our programmes
and our rustling wraps,
edging irresistibly closer
to His gleaming form,
loving Him
and wondering—past reach
of names by which we know Him—
wondering
what clock or calendar keeps Him
and Who He is.

THE PIONEER

– for all the lovely ladies –

*Ye are . . . the soft-flowing waters upon which must
depend the very life of all men . . . the breezes of spring
that are wafted over the world . . . Through you the countenance of the world hath been wreathed in smiles, and the
brightness of His light shone forth.*

Bahá'u'lláh

I

You will meet her anywhere,
the river, market, roadside, bus,
in Carcross, Nairobi, Liverpool, Duluth,
and the old girl will be smiling: she knows.
The sincere costume, the workworn hands, say little.
Satin or leather, the good, earnest face
belongs on a chocolate box, affirms,
could endorse nutritional causes on billboards
or in glossy magazines;
but she has far greater power
than Westinghouse or General Mills.
I warn you, she is dangerous.
In her bag there is a weapon
more potent than a gun.
If her lips move noiselessly
she is not litanizing her grievances
nor reading subway signs.
She carries more than recipes in her head.

II

It is fatal to speak to her,
no comment so mundane
she cannot bend it to her own design.
Chance a remark about the weather
and she may tell you of The Tempest,

leave you re-examining the roots of social unrest
and worrying about the fate of the House of Hapsburg.
She is not dismayed by headlines, calls them as her witness,
carries answers like neat balls of coloured yarn,
familiarly handled, spun of truth.
The mysteries are few and she lives with them companionably,
sibyl or saint, mystic or madwoman,
in ready-made dress and sensible shoes.

III

She has faced it, reconciled it all,
the whole human struggle,
the journey from the cave,
the love and the ashes,
the song and the blood,
the suffering, the stillborn, the greed,
ordered, forgiven, reconciled it all.
Her compassion spans eras and epochs,
finds room for Luther King, Lenin, Lao-tse,
all our lost leaders,
sorted, accommodated like the memory
of good or wayward children she has known; finds room
for the Aztec, Ibo, Tlingit, Vietnamese—
she might be one of them.
Fashions in indignation puzzle her.
It did not come as news that black is beautiful
(may be herself black);
knows Eskimos (or is one);
calls the Kalahari Bushmen brothers;
counts the Maoris as friends;
would have shielded the hapless
of Nagasaki, Warsaw, Buchenwald,
with her own body, if she could.
Long ago she wept and worked for causes

not then named,
knows symptom from disease
and is not resigned to evil.

IV

No, you do not imagine her authority;
dynasties might dissolve before it
or her concern melt mountains.
She is dangerous; she cannot be dismissed.
Your eloquent despair does not dissuade her:
*'The future is inestimably glorious,
and when one considers the life to come . . .'*
You will want to hurt her, destroy her dream,
but her words hang like heavy golden pears
and she knows your hunger.
Even as you strike she heals you
and in so doing heals herself.
You may crush her but she will not die—
she yields like grass
and is as indestructible.
She knows what you defend;
many times a midwife, she understands rebirth.
Your credentials don't impress her; she tinkers with souls.

V

Do not accept the invitation to her home
to meet her friend from Adelaide, Ṭihrán, Kaduna;
they are conspirators and drink from the same well.
Her own certitude is baked
into the cakes she serves with tea
tasting of her own contentment
that leaves you crazed,
thirsting forever for assurance.
Be warned, she is dangerous.

The moment is selected.
You will not see all heaven's angels,
all ancient good,
the very weight of history
rush to her support as she gathers breath
(her smile never more gentle)—
'Have you heard the Message of Bahá'u'lláh?'—
nor will you know that God Himself
throughout all worlds
gives ear to your reply.

I tell you, she is dangerous!

GRAVEYARDS ARE NOT MY STYLE
Thornton Chase
1847–1912

*This revered personage was the first Bahá'í in America
. . . his services will ever be remembered throughout
future ages and cycles. For the present his worth is not
known but in the future it will be inestimably dear . . .*

'Abdu'l-Bahá

Los Angeles: October 1912

That's a good woman you've got there, Paddy, a good
woman. I like the way she knows how to come and go, if you
follow me. Like her letting you have me round for a good meal

every Thursday and then setting out the stout and cards and slipping off to see her mother and leaving us to have a quiet game and talk. A man needs that, he gets lonely on his own.

I wish I weren't so clumsy with words, I'd like to tell your Rosie how much it's meant to me, coming here so often. I know she can tell by the way I dig into the food that I'm grateful and she probably thinks they starve me at my lodgings —Mrs D'Arcy, bless her, would die of shame if she thought Rosie believed that about her, and it isn't true because the old woman runs a good place and is a generous soul.

But it's more than that—it's the friendship you and Rosie give me and I'd like you to find a way of letting Rosie know I appreciate it. I know Rosie and I joke together and I like to make her laugh, but you know how I am with words when I try to be serious, they never come out the way I mean them. So try to let her know.

Since I left the old country I haven't made many friends— I'm not what you'd call a mixer—and you people treating me like family has meant a lot. Now with us, it's different; I can talk to another man, and a soul needs that—at least I do. And the truth is, Paddy, if it's all the same to you, I'd rather just sit a minute before we deal the cards because I want to speak my mind.

You see—well, I might as well come right out with it, like— I'm thinking of getting married—I mean I am going to get married—to Lil. Not right away, of course, but—well, I mean I asked her last week, on the nineteenth, to be exact— and she's accepted and now we're betrothed. No surprise to you, I guess, after all my talk about her. I knew the first time I met her at the shop that she was all I ever dreamed of. But there was the problem of religion—well, you must be sick of hearing about that, and all the fights we had, and her trying to make me see the light and crying at her failure. I guess I used hot words but you know how I stand. I mean, what would my people say, me coming to the new world and getting mixed up

41

in some queer religion—they might think of it as heathen. My poor old mother couldn't hold her head up in the village and the priest wouldn't take it lightly. As far as he's concerned the Church has a monopoly on God and he isn't one to divide the spoils with the competition. You should hear him go on about the Protestants—thinks they're the devil's own. Not that I'm religious or care what other people think, you understand, but it is a consideration, don't you see, and my mother in frail health. She wouldn't understand if Lil and I got married and had children and they weren't baptized. My mother's a simple good soul but fierce in her faith. In every letter she asks me have I been to Mass. Well, I never miss at Easter, as you know. She makes novenas for me too, God bless her.

And more than that, I'm jealous of Lil and I can't see why I'm not enough for her. Religion shouldn't come between people, as I see it. But my point is, why isn't it enough that we have each other? You know, sometimes I've even called for her with a drop on my breath just to have her take me as I am, to make her see it my way. A shameful thing for me to torment the poor girl, but dammit what's a man to do, and me half crazy with the love of her. And anyway religion is really a woman's business in the end; she has to give the children a decent start in life and some kind of training and see that they go to Church. But with Lil, religion's such an important matter—she's always trotting along to some meeting or other. Not that she doesn't invite me, but I'm uncomfortable with crowds and a man should be careful in choosing his friends. The truth of it being there are all kinds at these meetings—even Japanese. Not that I've anything against them, but what do you say to people like that? Words come hard with me at the best of times. And some of Lil's friends are comfortably off, you know, a little on the lace-curtain side, if you follow me. Not that they make an issue of it, but I feel a proper fool sitting on their fancy chairs, my fingers feeling like buttered sausages, balancing a dainty teacup and little sandwiches you could park in your cavity, and not having enough hands to hold it all, and worrying am I going to spill something on the Turkey carpet. And not a drop of spirits served, either, that might give a man courage. And all the talking that goes on and me not understanding the half of it.

'Why can't they have Churches like everybody else?' I say to Lil and she always answers 'Just *try* to understand'—as if I was working at *not* understanding—and then we usually wind up with me yelling, hot-tempered as I am, and her crying, and it's the longest time before she lets me hold her hand or peck her cheek and make our peace. And it leaves us both feeling sad and kind of hopeless and strained in our talk, like there was a sheet of glass between us.

Well, I've told you some of that before and maybe you've guessed that it wasn't all roses between us—that's why I brought her here just the once. She liked your Rosie a lot—I should tell Rosie that—and I saw them talking between them with their eyes over the teacups the way women do. But Lil would soon be dragging her off to meet her cut-glass-and-crystal friends. Maybe Rose would like that for all I know because they are good people, in truth, and they love my Lil and her being in a shop and me in a factory isn't held against us or anything—at least most of them really feel that way about us and the rest seem to be honestly trying to feel there's no difference. But I still can't see why Lil's friends don't just go to Church on Sunday like everybody else and say their prayers when they remember to, like the rest of us.

So after all the times I've told you how impossible it seemed between Lil and me—and sure there were some bad times— you must be wondering how we got it sorted out, our differences I mean; well, not really settled, but more or less, anyway. And to tell the truth I don't really know myself except that it began with Lil in tears—a change in pattern because it usually ends that way—and ended with me in tears. I don't mind admitting that to you, Paddy—I cried; blubbered like a baby I did, at the end. I thought I'd forgotten how to cry— a man outgrows that unless he's well into his cups and feeling homesick.

What happened was I picked Lil up at the shop to take her for a bit of an outing like we planned and she asked me to take her to the graveside of one of her friends—a nice old fellow named Thornton Chase I'd met and liked who died just the end of last month and was laid to rest all the way out in Inglewood. You know me, Paddy, I don't mind a good wake but I don't like funerals, and graveyards are not my style at all. Well, that was just a part of it. She wanted to be there because of the Master—that one she's always talking about with the name I can't pronounce. I find it easier to call him Master much as I dislike the term—it jars, foreign like. And he is a foreigner, as you know—you've heard me go on about him before and how he was in prison all that long while, and now he's come to America to see his followers; and after being in the East a bit he's come all the way to the West Coast and him an old man. Soon as she mentioned him I got a bit feisty. I landed in New York from the old country and came west too, I thought to myself, and I'll bet he didn't have to cross the country hard-timing and hoboing it like I did on my way west—thinking to myself you know. So I was a little heated up before I even opened my mouth and of course the words tripped me up and within minutes Lil was crying. The fact is, Paddy, I was jealous and I felt tricked and I knew there'd be a gathering with all Lil's friends, and speeches and sermons and hymns, and we'd not have a minute alone; and she'd been to Chase's funeral but a few weeks before. So I had good reason, in a way, for flying off the handle.

It was a kind of grim journey I can tell you but I got through it by being quiet. Even when Lil wanted to stop and buy flowers I didn't make a fuss. It wasn't the expense of them, you mind; it was the way she took so long selecting them that might have bothered me. But it didn't. It was watching the

careful way she chose them, like a bride picking out her bouquet you might say, that made me see how important this
meeting must be to her and I saw it through her eyes so to
speak. Meeting the Master must be one of the joys of her life,
says I to myself, and so I really tried to make it up to her by
speaking softly and telling her that I knew it was a special thing
for her to be seeing him for the first time—why, I'm sure she'd
follow him across the country if she had the money—and I told
her that I appreciated the fact that she would honour me by
allowing me to escort her to the meeting, and things like that.
And you know I meant it—it was all true—and she smiled and
her eyes took on that secret dreamy look they do and—well, I
never felt closer to her ever before.

Don't take offence if I don't drain my glass, Paddy,—you've
a kind heart and a generous hand—but I need my wits about
me to tell the next part and I swear I don't understand it
myself; but it would in truth seem a strange thing to be taking
a drop and talking about this at the same time, like cursing in
Church, do you see.

The thing is, it wasn't as bad as I thought it might be. Of
course, I'm always more at ease out of doors to begin with but
it was more than that. I suppose I have to say it was the
Master. What a fine old gentleman he is. Oddly dressed to be
sure, and looking like a bible figure in the stations of the cross;
and yet so natural, as though you always knew him. So I didn't
feel so out of place. The old gentleman walked to the grave
with great dignity and laid some flowers on it and took Lil's
flowers and the others' and scattered them, too, and spoke a
few simple words. Not the least unusual in a sense, but it was
the way he leaned down to the ground with tenderness like
a father bending to his dearest child to pat and comfort it. And
I thought to myself that I would give my life to have him look
at me that way. Well, says I to myself, this should tell Lil's
friends something—that this old man would come all this way
to do this simple thing at the grave and say what he did, that

Mr Chase would never be forgotten. The old gentleman seems to expect great things of Lil and her friends and no doubt they all well know it. I cannot bear to think they might disappoint him. If they broke his heart they'd hear from me about it, I swear it, Paddy, by all that's holy.

Then the Master turned to the people and said a few words to each so I hung back not wanting to spoil it for Lil. Her face was glowing and she looked so beautiful it took my breath away. And the old gentleman did the strangest thing—took her hand, as he had the others' too, and then reached for mine, drawing me forward. And there we were, him holding our hands in his, all three joined and touching, and he looked at each of us slowly and deeply and he said in English 'Yes'. Just '*Yes*'. It was eerie, as though he were answering a question —no, more than that—as though he were blessing us in marriage. I felt as though Lil and me were the only people in the world at that moment. And then he smiled a lovely smile and turned away.

We didn't speak on the way home—I guess we were both lost in thought; I know I was. And then suddenly I was sobbing my heart out with Lil patting my hand and saying 'It's all right, dearest, I know,'—like I was a child; and that's just how I felt to be sure. But I had been thinking of that look on the old gentleman's face when he was leaning toward the grave and wondering if ever I would be loved in that way by anyone. And I guess that's where the proposal came in because I couldn't help myself—I asked Lil if she loved me. And she said that she had always loved me, and that because she loved me through her love for God, as well as loving me for myself, her love would last through all this life and beyond it, too.

So I said to her—and it wasn't easy to say it and my eyes were still running with tears and my voice was cracking: 'Mavourneen, I want this for you if this is what you want. I want you to be his follower and I want you to be a good one, the best you can. And I'd be proud if you were. I don't know if I can be part of what you and your friends are doing, but I'll try to understand. All I can offer you is this: I know that this is good; I know he is a Holy Soul.'

'Well, my dear,' says she with one of those smiles that would melt a man's heart, 'that's a beginning, a very fine beginning.'

So you see, Paddy, that's how it was, the beginning, the real beginning with Lil and me. And now we're getting married. What puzzles me is that she's so calm about it all—goes about smiling and singing to herself as though she always knew it would come right.

There's no understanding women, is there, Paddy?

SIEGFRIED SCHOPFLOCHER
1877–1953

'When I first heard of the Bahá'í Faith, I said to myself:
"Freddie, if you get involved with this, it will cost you a
fortune." Well, I did. And it did.'

(remark attributed to him)

Ach, Freddie, mein lieber Kerl,
make light of it if you will,
malign your munificence,
we are not taken in.
But have your little joke;
assume the wry smile,
the classic shrug,
ask: 'What's a nice Jewish boy doing in a Cause like this?'
Extend the jest,
say: 'I surrendered profit and loss to Prophet and Laws'—
still, we are not deceived.

Freddie, you walked in
with eyes as open as your heart,

47

knew it to be the deal beyond compromise;
survived the imagery
accommodated to nightingales and roses
endured our pious vagaries and poor arithmetic
loved the *goyim*
were loved
made of heart and palm a purse and emptied both
and learned (or always knew)
that God does not strike bargains.

Tsk! Freddie,
splendidly generous,
your private charities betrayed you;
we only pretended to accord
the anonymity you sought.
What man builds a shelter for mankind?
The Mother of Temples casts no greater shadow
than that of your humility;
how can you hide from us?
Daring to have loved us
you must suffer now our love,
and having given all
accept our gift,
your modesty a magnet to our admiration.

Ach, Freddie, mein lieber Freund,
make light of it if you will—
you, inspired spendthrift,
lavish legator;
we your grateful heirs
left solvent in the knowledge
that we need fear
only bankruptcy of God.
Ach, Freddie!
Ach, mein lieber Freund!

VERDICT OF A HIGHER COURT

In the interest of posterity we are asked
to review the case. The dossier is before
us. Shall we get on with it then?

Transcript of Proceedings of the District
Court of the Fourth Judicial District,
State of Minnesota, held on the 8th day
of August in the year of Our Lord one
thousand nine hundred and . . .

Well, so that's how it is. Not yet a
decade into the twentieth century and
life is just a bowl of cherries. Live on
your wits and cover all the exits.

The prisoner, Fred Mortensen, will rise
while the Court pronounces sentence.

Hot-shot, aren't you, Fred? All set to
highstep it into the years of the Greatest
War on Earth and then to go twenty-
three-skidooing into the Jazz Age—if
you live that long—with a bottoms-up-
boys-for-tomorrow-we-may-die and all
that razzmatazz.

In considering the evidence before it the
Court has given due weight to the
extreme youth of the Defendant . . .

About twenty-one or so, are you, Fred?
But then, mugs must make an early
start if they are to amount to
anything—with a down-the-hatch-

fellows and a chug-a-lug-a-lug and don't
take any wooden nickels.

Before passing sentence the Court
expresses regret that one of such
obvious potential should have launched
himself upon a course of action that can
only blight his future, brand him an
enemy of the public good and break his
mother's heart . . .

So you found yourself in prison with a
gee-there-ain't-no-justice and a blast-it-
I've-been-framed? Well, Fred let's
review the facts.

Although he has taken the path of a
common ruffian the Court appeals to
whatever tender feelings may yet stir
within the Defendant's bosom . . .

Easy does it, Fred. Florid oratory is a
hazard to which most Judges display
little resistance. But we take it you will
concede that even tough guys have
feelings? Remember how you cried a
little in the darkened theatre during one
of Mary Pickford's films and had to
quickly conceal it from the gang with an
improvised coughing spasm? And how a
lump came to your throat each time you
heard Eva Tanguay sing 'Mother'?

At an age when the Defendant's mother
is entitled to his comfort and assistance,
she faces the tragic and humiliating
consequences of her son's iniquitous

50

conduct. The Court is satisfied on the
evidence that the Defendant's mother is
an upright, decent, God-fearing . . .

Patience, Fred, he's only doing his job.
Admittedly he does get a bit carried
away. But the docket is light today and
his gout is under control and perhaps he
is pontificating out of boredom. But
maybe the old boy has a point there.
We confront you with your own
testimony:

'My dear mother had done
everything in her power to make me a
good boy. I have but the deepest love
for her and my heart has often been sad
when thinking how she must have
worried for my safety as well as my
future well-being. Through it all and in
a most wonderful way, with godlike
patience, she hoped and prayed that her
boy would find the road which leads to
righteousness and happiness. But
environment proved a great barrier to
her aspirations and every day in every
way I became tougher and tougher . . . '

Come now, Fred, is that how tough
guys talk?

The Court is charged with the
responsibility of protecting society from
those who wilfully disregard its laws.
Equally, the Court has the responsibility
of imposing sanctions which will afford
the maximum opportunity of moral
rehabilitation . . .

Relax, Fred, and don't let the high-flown language get you down. Look at it this way—the judiciary has a vocabulary just as specialized, though somewhat less colourful, than that of budding thugs. But on the subject of rehabilitation, that came later through a man with gentle eyes. Remember Bert Hall, Fred? One of the finest lawyers in Minnesota, it was said, and a remarkable human being. Do you recall what the Hennepin County Bar Association said of Albert Hall?

'He was essentially the poor man's lawyer; no client was too mean, nor was his cause too small, but that Bert Hall gave him his untiring and unstinted effort.'

Well, you were a mean one, all right, and whatever had been your cause you were presented with a new one, a cause of intimidating magnitude, as the Judge might say. Let us read into the record your own words:

'Albert Hall told me, hour after hour, about the great love of 'Abdu'l-Bahá. Honestly, I often wondered then what Mr. Hall meant when he talked so much about God's love, Bahá'u'lláh's love, 'Abdu'l-Bahá's love, love for the Covenant, and so on. I was bewildered. Still, I kept returning, and I wondered why. Later I realized it was the power of the Holy Spirit drawing one who wished to be drawn.'

Fine talk for a tough guy, Fred!

It is lamentable that one of the
Defendant's age should have amassed,
shall we say, so impressive a record of
criminal activity . . .

Euphemism is the backbone of
courtroom wit, Fred. One gets used to
it, though developing an appreciation of
verbosity is another matter. For
instance, 'Learned Judge' is sometimes a
euphemism for old windbag. But let us
hear him out.

. . . disturbing the peace, using abusive
language, harassing members of
oppressed minority groups, being drunk
and disorderly, assault, theft, escaping
from custody, aiding the escape of a
fellow prisoner, violating parole,
resisting arrest . . .

Well, all that must have kept you pretty
busy, Fred. But one impulse you could
neither resist nor arrest, remember? Will
you disavow your own incriminating
words:

'I felt urged by the Holy Spirit to go to
see 'Abdu'l-Bahá at Green Acre, Maine.
When I heard the rumour that He might
not come west, I immediately
determined to go and see Him. So I left
Minneapolis for Cleveland where I
attended a convention of printers for a
few days. But I became so restless I
could not stay for adjournment. As my
finances were low, I of necessity must

hobo my way to Green Acre . . . '

We note that euphemism is not the
exclusive indulgence of the Court. But
to continue:

'I rode the rods . . . '

Now that's more like it:

' . . . to Buffalo, then to Boston, then to
Portsmouth. I was exceedingly happy. A
boat ride, a streetcar ride, and there I
was, at the gate of Paradise . . . '

An interesting destination for one of
your proclivities!

Do you remember first entering His
presence and His asking you whether
you had a pleasant journey? Let us
examine your own account of this:
'Question: "Did you have a
pleasant journey?"
Of all the questions I wished to avoid
this was the one! I dropped my
gaze to the floor—and again He put the
question. I lifted my eyes to His eyes
and His were as two sparkling jewels
which seemed to look into my very
depths. I knew He knew and I must tell.
I answered: "I did not come as people
generally do, who come to see You."
Question: "How did you come?"
Answer: "Riding under and on top of
the railway trains."
Question: "Explain how?" '

And you explained while His eyes
twinkled. He gave you fruit, kissed both

your cheeks and touched to His lips the
soiled hat you had worn. And after that,
at His invitation, you spent a week in
His presence at Malden.

What are we to make of that, Fred?

The Court invites the Defendant to
consider that in a land of limitless
opportunity one of his age might, by
pursuing the proper course, make his
mark on its history . . .

Restrain yourself again, Fred. There
might be something in this. There has
been entered in the record, and marked
Exhibit A, a Tablet addressed to you
from Ramleh, Egypt, bearing date 12
September 1913. The signature is that of
'Abdu'l-Bahá:

'That trip of thine from Minneapolis to
Green Acre will never be forgotten. Its
mention will be recorded eternally in
books and works of history . . . '

Annexed to Exhibit A is a copy of *God
Passes By*. We are asked to note the
reference on page 290. Let it be so
noted.

The Prosecuting Attorney dwelt at
considerable length . . .

He means excruciating length, Fred.

. . . on the circumstances in which the
Defendant was apprehended at
gunpoint, in a barrage of police bullets,
his capture being accomplished as a

55

result of breaking both legs in scaling a
wall while attempting to elude the
police, and has repeatedly emphasized
that for four years the Defendant was a
fugitive from justice . . .

Easy, there, Fred. Why not relax and
read Exhibit A?

The Court cannot view lightly the
Defendant's contempt for the rules
which must govern a civilized society. It
emerges from the evidence before the
Court that the pattern of the
Defendant's behaviour is determinedly
antisocial . . .

He does turn a vivid phrase, doesn't he?
Fulgurant, it might be said. We toss
that word in to see whether we still have
the knack—we abandoned
grandiloquent rhetoric a long time ago;
too time-consuming. Actually it has
never been determined whether Judges
are expected by lawyers to talk like that
or only think they are.

But speaking of patterns emerging from
the evidence—which seems to be the
point the good Judge was
making—another pattern emerges. Will
you deny that over the long haul you
laboured diligently—sorry, it is so easy
to lapse into the jargon; but the
following words mean just what they
convey—for the establishment of the
Kingdom of God on earth and that

until the eve of your death on 13 June 1946 you were so engaged?

Tendered as Exhibit B is an outline of your service on the Bahá'í Temple Unity, your pioneering to Montana, your service as a national travelling teacher and as a member of the Chicago Bahá'í community, your preparations for a journey to Austria, to name a few. Let the Exhibit be marked.

Although ever inclined toward leniency, on the basis of what has been adduced before it the Court must be satisfied in considering the question of sentence that the interest of justice will be fully served. With that in mind it is the opinion of this Court . . .

And yes, one final piece of testimony. Let there be marked as Exhibit C a document described as a cablegram sent from Haifa in June 1946 to members of your family:

'Grieve passing beloved Fred. Welcome assured Abhá Kingdom by Master . . . His name forever inscribed Bahá'í history.'

The evidence, we submit, is irrefutable. Let the verdict be recorded: Guilty of spiritual recidivism.

Next case.

THE COURIER

O Son of Love! Thou art but one step away from the . . .
celestial tree of love. Take thou one pace and with the next
advance into the immortal realm and enter the pavilion of
eternity.

Bahá'u'lláh
The Hidden Words

How many steps, Salmán, Salmán,
To world of God from world of man?
How far, how far, untutored fool,
From Land of Tá to 'Akká's Jewel?

Coarse of mien and taint of breath,
In each pace might have lain your death.
Companioned by lone wheeling bird
You brought the lovers Love's Own Word.

How lonely were your many miles
Fuelled by onions and friends' smiles?
If dust leapt up to kiss your sole
Had it not guessed and blessed your goal?

To hostile eyes not once revealed
The treasure in your hat concealed.
Behold, a stricken world knows now
What safely rode above your brow.

By some, scorned as unlettered oaf,
How educated was your troth!
So trained to scan, your simple heart
Chose who attained, who stood apart.

How many are the steps that bring
The loutish vassal to his King?
Tell this halt, fugacious son
In what step is the soul's home won?

How many steps, Salmán, Salmán,
To world of God from world of man?
Lend him your courage who has none
And treads all paths save one. *Save one!*

EARLY WINE

*Thomas Breakwell, the first English Bahá'í, accepted the
Faith in his twenties in the summer of 1901 as a result of
meeting May Ellis Bolles. Startled by a mystical experience which followed upon their first meeting he asked her
whether she thought he was parting with his senses. 'No,'
she replied, 'you are just becoming sane.' He made a pilgrimage to 'Akká not long thereafter and within a short
time died of consumption. 'Abdu'l-Bahá revealed in his
honour a eulogy of unparalleled beauty.*

For you was May detained that you come sane
And in the wind hear *Christ has come again*,
In your life's doomed May, in the oblivious air
Of inattentive Paris. What mute prayer
Brought you to the waiting singular door
Of one—of all the servants—frailest; core
And mother-soul of Europe?

My Lord, I believe . . .

Now could your cask decline and you not grieve;
But 'Akká gained, the lover will exclaim:

Let life endure that I taste more of pain!

Your Spring's brief yield, love-wine immortals drink;
None mourns to see the slender goblet sink.

> *O Breakwell, O my dear one!*
> *Thy Lord hath verily singled thee out*
> *for His love . . .*

First grape of Albion, fruit of fragile vine,
Not ours to stay from King this early wine.
The pain-perfected vessel God lets slip,
But first had raised that sweet draught to His lip.

PART TWO: GLIMPSES OF 'ABDU'L-BAHÁ

adapted from the diary of Juliet Thompson

No word of mine would suffice to express how instantly the revelation of 'Abdu'l-Bahá's hopes, expectations and purpose . . . electrified the minds and hearts of those who were privileged to hear Him, who were made the recipients of His inestimable blessings . . . I can never hope to interpret adequately the feelings that surged within those heroic hearts as they sat at their Master's feet . . . I can never pay sufficient tribute to that spirit of unyielding determination which the impact of a magnetic personality and the spell of a mighty utterance kindled in the entire company of those returning pilgrims, these consecrated heralds of the Covenant of God . . .

Shoghi Effendi

GLIMPSES OF 'ABDU'L-BAHÁ

Adapted from the Diary of Juliet Thompson

'Akká: July 1909

We drive along a wide white beach.
Sea waves curl about our carriage wheels,
Camels approach on the sand,
cloaked Bedouins attending.
Palm trees in a long, long line
and in the distance domes and flat roofs,
dazzling white.

Walls.
Walls within walls.
Menacing walls.
Tall, prison-like, chalk-white houses,
leaning together, rising towards a rift of sky,
slits of barred windows set here and there
in their forbidding fronts.
Streets so narrow that our wheels
graze buildings on either side—
streets sometimes bridged by houses
meeting in an arch at their second stories.
Pervading us,
a sense of the divine joy towards which we travel,
here in the Holy City, the New Jerusalem.

Before us, suddenly, a broad expanse:
a garden,
the seawall,
the sea,
and then the Master's door.
Too soon we have arrived,
too suddenly, and unprepared.

He bursts upon us like the sun
with His joyous greeting:

Welcome! Welcome!

His effulgence strikes me blind!

Are you well? Are you happy?

I cannot speak.

He takes my hand in His—
in His so mysterious hand—
delicately-made, steely-strong,
currents of life streaming from it:

Your heart, your spirit, speak to Me.
I hear. I know.
Do not think your services are
unknown to Me. I have seen.
I have been with you.
I know them all.
For these you are accepted
in the Kingdom.

My services! Their pitiful smallness!
And my lack of love!
Pierced by shame I cry:
'Forgive my failures!'

Be sure of this. Be sure of this.

My knees yield; my heart draws me down to His feet.

Later, my eyes upon His white-robed Figure,
I listen as He dictates Tablets,
see Him pace about a room grown suddenly too small.
A force born of the energy of God—
restless, uncontainable—
spills from Him.
The earth cannot contain Him,

nor yet the universe.
When He pauses by the window I sense His spirit,
free as the Essence Itself,
brooding over regions far distant,
looking deep into hearts
at the uttermost ends of the earth,
consoling their secret sorrows,
answering the whispers of far-off minds.
Often in His leonine pacing
He gives me a long, grave glance.
And once He smiles at me.
He smiles at me!

Thonon-les-Bains, Lake Geneva: August, 1911

A great white hotel, set amid oleander,
flanked by mountains overhung with clouds.
Beyond the green terrace and marble balustrade,
the lake.
In the halls and through the grounds
the artificial, dull-eyed people
stroll and chatter.
Silently,
majestically,
unrecognized but not unfelt,
He passes among them,
the cream robe billowing,
light glinting in His silver hair.
The metallic voices break off.
The shadowed eyes lift and follow,
lighted for a moment with wonder.
His presence is an affirmation,
stirring them to recall their lost vision
of a higher world and their own beauty.
The eloquent assertion of His silence!
His magnetic power!
His holy sweetness!

At a country inn I see Him
in a half-circle of children,
girdled with children, festooned with them,
waist-deep in children with violets to sell,
the small ones, themselves a bouquet,
pressing about Him, waving the purple clusters,
their faces raised with grave astonishment,
His own a benediction as He bends
to buy their blooms, buy all their blooms,
drawing from His pocket handfuls of francs,
giving to each child bountifully.
They beg for more.
'Don't let them impose!'
At the edge of the swaying crescent,
a newcomer, the smallest,
stares up in awe,
timid as a fawn:

> *To this little one I have not given . . .*

And the Master gave.

On the road back, suddenly, spectacularly,
a waterfall,
rolling from a great height,
scattering diamonds as it froths down a
black precipice.
Full of excitement He hurries forward, alone,
to sit in silence at the very edge,
the swirling water far below.
I see Him in profile,
kingly against the cascade,
intense rapture on His upturned face,
and my tears flow.
After a time, smiling:

> *If I come to America, will you
> invite Me to see such waterfalls?*

I promise Niagara!
'But surely, my Lord,
Your coming to America does not depend
upon my invitation!'

> *My invitation to America will be
> the unity of the believers!*

A heavenly day of charming informality,
taking tea,
He talking gaily or tenderly,
taking little notice of me.
But in spite of this I glimpse something vaster
than before,
feel a new awareness of His unearthly power,
His divine sweetness.

Coming upon Him as He stands talking with a friend,
the sweetness of His love,
that celestial radiance,
again bring tears:
If He never gave me so much as a word,
if He never glanced my way,
just to see that sweetness shining before me,
I would follow Him on my knees,
crawling behind Him in the dust forever!

New York: 11 April 1912

April 11th! Oh day of days!
I awaken before daybreak with a singing heart,
the moon's waning sliver
framed low in my windowpane.
I hasten to the pier.
The morning is crystal clear, sparkling.
I have a sense of its being Easter—of lilies,
almost seen, blooming at my feet.

A mist settles over the harbour but at last,
at last, I see a phantom ship,
an epoch-making ship,
coming closer, closer, ever more substantial,
till it swims into the light, a solid thing.
He sends His love and asks us to disperse—
we are all to meet at four.
Obedience is overruled by love: three of us
conceal ourselves and wait.
Stepping into the limousine,
the Master turns and smiles at us!
Three frozen statues dissolve in that bestowal,
no love-born child-prank ever so rewarded.
Oh the coming of that Presence!
The mighty commotion of it!
The hearts almost suffocate with joy and the eyes
burn with tears at the stir of that step!
Our skyscrapers had delighted Him:

The Minarets of the West!

What divine irony!

New York: 19 April

He shines in white and ivory,
His face a lighted lamp
illumining the Bowery Mission:

> *Tonight I am very happy*
> *for I have come here to meet My friends.*
> *I consider you My relatives,*
> *My companions, and I am your*
> *comrade . . .*

A sodden and grimy procession
streams down the aisle,
perhaps three hundred men in single file—

derelicts, failures, broken forms, blurred faces—
and here 'The Servant' receiving each outcast
as His beloved child.
Into each palm, as He clasps it,
He presses His little gift of silver—
just a symbol and the price of a bed.
None is shelterless this night
and many find a shelter in His heart;
I see it in their faces,
and in His face bent to theirs.

We drive up Broadway, aglitter with electric signs.
He speaks of them, smiling, much amused.
'It is marvellous to be driving
through all this light
by the side of the Light of lights.'

> *This is only the beginning. We will*
> *be together in all the worlds of God.*
> *You cannot realize here what that means.*
> *You cannot imagine it. You can form*
> *no conception here in this elemental*
> *world of what it is to be with Me in*
> *the Eternal Worlds.*

New York: 5 June

I am to paint His portrait!
Surprise, dismay, fear, joy, gratitude, flood me.
He sits before me in a dark corner,
His black 'abá melting into the background.
I quail.

> *I want you to paint My servitude*
> *to God.*

Only the Holy Spirit could do so, no human hand.

'Pray for me, or I am lost.
I implore You, inspire me!'

> *I will pray, and as you are*
> *doing this only for the sake of God,*
> *you will be inspired.*

Fear falls away.
It is as though another sees through my eyes,
works through my hand.
Rapture takes possession of me.
My hand is directed in a sort of furious precision.
The points, the planes in the matchless face
are so clear
my hand cannot keep pace with the clarity
of my vision.
Freely, in ecstasy, I paint as I never have before.
In half an hour the foundation is perfect.

Once, bidding Him rest, I find I cannot paint—
what I see is too sacred, too formidable.
He sits still as a statue, eyes closed,
infinite peace on that chiseled face,
a God-like calm and grandeur in His erect head.
Suddenly, with a great flash, like lightning,
He opens His eyes.
The room seems to rock
like a storm-tossed ship
in the power released!

West Englewood: 29 June

A luminescent summer day
green countryside, and He our host.
The Unity Feast has ended and the darkness
settles in, gently smudging the outline
of the mighty trees.

Many of us linger, unable to wrench ourselves away.
Cricket songs—the scent of grass—
a breathless expectancy in the soft, warm air.
He sits in a chair on the top step of the porch,
some of us surrounding Him.
Below, dotting the lawn, on either side of the path,
sit others, the light summer skirts of the women
spread out on the grass,
lighted tapers in their hands.
In the dark, in their filmy dresses,
they become great pale moths,
and the burning tips of the tapers,
flickering fireflies.
Knowing our thirst, He speaks to us again,
words of consuming tenderness.
Rising, He starts down the path, still talking,
passing between the weightless, dim figures
with their lighted candles,
talking, still talking, till He reaches the road.
He turns and we no longer see Him.
Even then His words float back to us,
the liquid Persian,
and the beautiful, quivering translation,
the sound and the echo hovering and drifting,
an exquisite note almost unbearably held:

>   *Peace be with you. I will pray for you.*

Oh that voice that speaks out of His invisibility,
when He has passed beyond our sight!
May I always remember.
May I always remember and hear that voice!

New York: 5 December

The last morning.
I stand at His door, my brimming eyes

fastened upon that divine Figure
as He moves about the room.
Taking my hand, He consoles me:

> *Remember, I am with you always.*
> *Bahá'u'lláh will be with you always . . .*

And then the ship, and His last spoken message,
the Master pacing the crowded cabin
filled with flowers
and broken-hearted friends:

> *. . . your efforts must be lofty.*
> *Exert yourselves with heart and soul*
> *so that perchance through your efforts*
> *the light of Universal Peace may*
> *shine. . . that all men may become*
> *as one family. . . It is My hope*
> *that you may become successful in*
> *this high calling, so that like*
> *brilliant lamps you may cast light*
> *upon the world of humanity and*
> *quicken and stir the body of existence*
> *like unto a spirit of life.*
> *This is eternal glory.*
> *This is everlasting felicity.*
> *This is immortal life.*
> *This is heavenly attainment.*
> *This is being created in the image*
> *and likeness of God. . .*

I sit opposite Him at a little distance,
weeping quietly.
At each parting I was left with the hope of
another meeting, and now my question must be
answered or I shall have no peace.
'Will I see You again, my Lord?'

> *This is My hope.*

'But still You don't tell me, my Lord.
Not knowing, I feel hopeless.'

> *You must not feel hopeless.*

Only that.
That is all He said to me.

It is death to leave the ship.
I remain on the pier, in the grey light,
with the impervious, stolid pigeons
and the anguished gulls.
Tears blur my eyes.
Through them I see the Master
in the midst of the throng,
waving a patient hand to us.

It waves and waves—
that beautiful patient hand—
till the Figure is lost to sight.

Haifa: 9 December 1956: In Memoriam

> *Deplore loss much loved greatly admired
> Juliet Thompson outstanding exemplary
> handmaid 'Abdu'l-Bahá. Over half century
> record manifold meritorious services
> embracing concluding years Heroic
> opening decades Formative Age Bahá'í
> Dispensation won her enviable position
> glorious company triumphant disciples
> beloved Master Abhá Kingdom. Advise hold
> memorial gathering Mashriqu'l-Adhkár pay
> befitting tribute imperishable memory one
> so wholly consecrated Faith Bahá'u'lláh
> fired such consuming devotion Centre His
> Covenant.   Shoghi*

PART THREE:

LINES FROM A PERSIAN

NOTEBOOK

The cause of the rejection and persecution of the Báb was in its essence the same as that of the rejection and persecution of the Christ.
> Shoghi Effendi
> Introduction to *The Dawn-Breakers*

DR CORMICK DECIDES

Tabríz, 1848

Well, not an auspicious beginning to this day,
the tea undrinkable
and Aḥmad in a sulk
for one of those mysterious reasons
no mere Englishman could understand—
an advantage we unfeeling barbarians have,
I suppose, over these excessively sensitive Persians.

And the beastly report to be written
of that curious interview.
I have little heart for that.
How to find the balance between my observations
and what the ears of power might hope to hear
about the poor wretch,
or to know the disposition of my Persian colleagues
and what might sway them from detachment
to a devious or dictated course?
They could be agents of an ill-wisher.
At best they are Western only when it serves them to be.
Sane or mad, the authorities will bring about this death
if that be their wish.
Exercises in futility weary me;
the examination I suspect was merely
a token nod towards justice,
some aspect of the unfathomable and
interminable face-saving ceremony.
Can one ever understand their ways?

As for my part, what can I say?
I found myself admittedly disposed
most kindly toward the Báb—
his courtesy and dignity of bearing struck me much.

Attractive, mild of manner and
melodious of voice—nothing offensive there.
I might remark upon his delicacy of stature
and his tender youth—but what relevance has that?

No surprise that he,
knowing the purpose of our attendance upon him,
should have been loth to answer our questions,
merely regarding us with a gentle look,
continuing with his chanting—
hymns or devotionals, I suppose.
And this the one who claims to be
the Mahdí of the Mussulmen!
What to make of it all?

I shall weight my report in his favour, no doubt;
I see no other way. It would please me well
to think his life were spared. 'Frankly,' I shall say,
'I am impelled in the circumstances to recommend
the utmost leniency in this difficult matter . . .'
The words will come as I apply myself to it.

I cannot take sides in these affairs, of course,
and it would appear to be of appalling significance
that this young man should have subverted
the religion of the realm and convulsed
the populace with his cry: 'I am the Promised One.'
The Promised One indeed!
Well, no doubt he believes it.
An infernal nuisance, the whole affair.
And what to make of his assertion that
Europe will espouse his cause—
the intensity with which he regarded me as he said it?
Extraordinary, really. Most extraordinary.
I suppose my part in it is over and
I shan't see him again.

One wonders what might become of such a fellow.
Perhaps, of course, it's just another tempest in a teapot.
Ah well, with the Persians, it is always something.

Today—yes—
I think, today, the grey cravat.

A CRIMSON RAIN

And there shall be martyrs and saints . . .
T. S. Eliot
Chorus No. 6 from *The Rock*

I

Fort of Ṭabarsí
Mázindarán
May 1849

His head now cushioned against my breast,
I see how lightly his closed lashes shadow the soft cheek;
even in death my friend is beautiful.
He has met his end with a startled, gentle courage,
his recumbent form assumes the chaste and artless grace
of a child or dancer. So must his mother have held him,
and so wept, but wept for his bright promise.
With what joy would I have led him to his wedding
in a season less sanguine. Never, now,
will I dandle his gurgling children on my knee.
Never again will we fatigue the aghast stars
with our chanting and our laughter,
or huddle, chilled and yawning, as the last candle fails,

talking of honour.
These slender hands—do they supplicate
for the accustomed book and pen?
My tears do not erase the bruises.

How young, how pale he is!
This pallor is not earned by dissipation.
What had this sheltered scholar need know
of soldiering or death?
It was no feat to kill him.
What resistance might this frail vessel offer
or rage this bosom store? That delicate
shattered cage held no aptitude for hate.

See how timidly his blood now stains my tunic.
Comrade-in-Faith, would that this thin, reluctant trickle
might brand your name upon my flesh for all to know.
His name? Ah world! you would not care,
nor does he need your tawdry accolades.
Lavish them upon your athletes,
your fawning princes, your debased divines.
God keeps his name! And I, his friend,
shall keep it while I draw breath, though
that may not be long—Ḥusayn felled,
Quddús injured, our number dwindling.
But in this moment this death, this name, are known,
and God's moments are eternal.

The siege resumes, and now I fight for two.
Weeping, I leave you, my gallant-in-God,
even my grief sacrificed to this awful hour.

Seminal your death, little brother—
all our deaths.
O Persia! Pitiless Persia! One day you shall,
you shall know what you have done.

Though they go mad they shall be sane.
Dylan Thomas
Death Shall Have No Dominion

II

Fort of Kh̲ájih
Nayríz
Autumn 1850

Yes, certainly I knew him.
The man was a fool, I say,
and worse, a heretic.
Ask the townspeople, they all revile him.
I grant you he knew the Qur'án well
and once had my respect. He was honest in his dealings
and had honour. But to disgrace his family as he did,
and at his age!
Life was comfortable for him—
small merchants do well enough—
and he threw everything away,
bewitched by a green turban.
God spare us the snares of senility
and keep us safe from the persuasion of roses and women!
Ah, my friends, let us pray the years will bring us wisdom,
if not piety—too much to hope for, eh?—
and a dignified death.

He fell with the fort, of course,
his head carried aloft through the street
with the others'—
the grey beard tinged gruesomely scarlet—
while the crowd jeered. I daresay the vultures dined well.
His brother turned to me for comfort, sick with shame.
'He was a fool', I told him; what more could I say?
A degrading, grisly end, but just what he deserved.
I am a reasonable man and give religion its due

but it excites unseemly passion.
Certainly one can hope God winks at human foibles,
but to flout authority and violate the Faith is madness.
God and His Prophet deal with those!

I dreamed for long of the head,
the expression curiously peaceful—
one might almost say smiling.
I confess it rather rattled me.
But that was last summer and life again is normal.
You see, it came to nothing, as these things will.
Come, let us enjoy our tea;
why spoil a pleasant day with talk of this?
One has said it all in saying he was mad.

    Well, now, have you ever seen such pomegranates!
    So large and red, and yet so strangely bitter;
    I, at least, have no taste for them.
    Is it age?

——

    . . .pathetic scenes [followed] upon the division of the
inhabitants of Zanján into two distinct camps, by order of
its governor . . . which dissolved ties of worldly interest
and affection in favour of a mightier loyalty. . .

Shoghi Effendi
God Passes By

III

Fort of 'Alí-Mardán Khán
Zanján
December 1850

In this interval of silence, mother,
we count our dead or find solace with our loved ones,
and so I write to you with but faint hope my words
will reach you. The scribe assures me that a

kinsman may find a way to carry this beyond the walls.
How weary these stones must be of our long struggle here!
It has not been easy—food and fodder in short supply,
brackish water—and the cold is constant.
Death and suffering are now familiar, but still
I am not reconciled; only my own death will cause me to forget
what I have seen.

But I do not forget you, mother dear, no matter what befalls.
Twice we are divided, by marriage and by faith—
you must observe my father's will,
and I my husband's;
and as I adopt this as my own will,
are we thrice separated then?
Oh! may we all drown in the will of God!
The times twist us but behind these walls I love you.
Though heaven be in upheaval let me reach across
and speak—there may not be another time for this!
Attend me with your heart, mother,
for I carry your grandchild
and hope this news will bring you joy.
One day you may receive us with smiles.
So, you see, life continues, even here.

Rumours will have reached you. Too large for reality
seem the people here—
even the women garb as men and seize the sword.
It is all too strange and troubling.
But God inspires what He will
in this great day. You may find me somewhat changed
but you will know me—what has the governor's decree to do
with our love? Am I not still your child, your *jigar-gúshih?*
Offer me your *ḥalvá* and you will know!
I am better suited to prepare the samovar
or dawdle among the girls over some light task
with chitchat and melon seeds
than to live in the camp of heroes;

83

yet God has brought me here. And, yes, your own good life has
set me on this path.
These fingers which you guided towards *guldúzí*
now tend the wounded. I am slow.
My friends show great patience
with my awkward ways; they give, I think,
more than my share of food.
I have cut my hair to bind the muskets
but find dressing it is simpler.
My hands which were your pride when daintily
patterned with henna
now wear a more vital, deeper dye—
but still they would hold you to my breast.
And with it all, your place in my heart is unchanged,
nor must you worry. I move with care, watchful of my trust.

The one called Ḥujjat is here
and the enemy will soon be upon us—
once more the noise and the blood.
Birth cannot be soundless or without stain.
Though much and many will it wash away
I do not fear this crimson rain
for every drop must tell
and all shall be fed of the heavy harvest.

If I live I shall again take up this letter
and, if not, may you one day rejoice, mother,
that mine was not an idle death.

I ask little in a world that shows slight mercy
but this I beg of you:
Speak gently to my father and win him back to me!

jigar-gushih—a term of endearment, equivalent to 'your heart's remnant'.
guldúzí—a kind of embroidery.

84

COMMAND PERFORMANCE

Ablaze like a theatre,
voice upraised in song,
one comes dancing in the dust,
costumed in candles,
his performance lighted
with flames fed
by his own flesh.

The crowd jeers,
not knowing this to be
solo by royal command,
spectacle beyond applause;
this the music of *Am I not your Lord?*
this the choreography of *Yea verily thou art!*

A MOUSE AMONG HAWKS

*The women and children were captured and subjected to
brutalities which no pen dare describe.*

> Nabíl
> *The Dawn-Breakers*

Nayríz, June 1850

Qamar is a beauty, her skin unusually fair;
it did not go well with her after they seized us
and we were given as playthings to the troops,
the soldiers drunk and brutal,
mocking us in our disgrace.
God alone knows our sufferings,
the indignities we bore.

I was spared much, being older,
the cast of my eye thought an evil mark.
But Qamar, unmarried, slender,
with the quick grace of a gazelle,
lovely as the moon whose name she bears—
what can I say? She was a mouse among hawks.
Her virtue and shyness incited them
to shameful conduct.
One officer singled her out for his attentions
and won her stern rebuke.
Glancing at the lance on which
her father's severed head was held aloft
she called: 'Beloved Father, had you
thought me worthy of so brave a suitor?'
Even some of the men tittered at her audacity.
The humiliated officer struck her face and
turned her over to the regiment.
For all her tears and pleading
they showed no mercy. She was silent then,
woodenly compliant, as if removed to another world,
as they led her away.
I cannot think it gave them pleasure.

When it grew dark she crept to me,
bruised and sobbing. I freed her wrists
and wiped the men's spittle from her face,
rocked her in my arms till she grew calm.
We chanted softly, clinging together.
Here and there a child whimpered,
a sleeper cried out. In the distance
the men revelled, cursed and made lewd boasts.
I felt that God saw our misery, heard our prayer.

Later we slept, though fitfully,
cramped and crowded as we were.
The night was chill and we had not been given rations.

When I awakened the sky was growing light.
Qamar stood with her back to me and
with a small blade was hacking off her hair
which fell soundlessly in black drifts to her feet.
Her hands worked in measured precision across her scalp
among the jagged tufts and bristles.
'Qamar! Your lovely hair!' I gasped.
She turned then to silence me
and I saw the oozing stripes her nails
had raked across her cheeks and breast—these
she'd daubed with mud to staunch the bleeding.
As I again cried out in horror
she advanced toward me like one moving in a trance.
'Rejoice for me,' she said softly.
'Now only God may find me pleasing.'

THE CONJURER

These eyes have gazed upon His countenance . . .
Mírzá Muḥammad-'Alíy-i-Zunúzí (Anís)

Tabríz, 1850

It is the way of boys
to lie brooding in their shaded rooms
languidly conjuring the heroic images
or the nippled voluptuousness
by which budding men
assert their dreams
and annul the dull existence

of the practical furniture
that sombrely clamours
to define their life by diminution;
their way
to weep over Ḥáfiz or Rumí
for our fleet hour,
the mortality of roses,
song so soon ended, and
to sigh for the fragile throbbing flesh
which can yet but imagine love
nor know its tyranny.

It is the need of parents
to deny these tremulous flights
which in anarchial, merciless privacy
annihilate our lives
disclaim our features
and demolish our decisions;
our need
to call the youth
to the substantial meal,
the headlines of the day,
the unpaid bill
and the educated compromise.
We who are good at sums and court no scandal
foresee the poem forgotten,
have known the tender yielding lips
and slender slanting thigh
coarsened, grown flaccid
with boredom and trivia.

And so, Anís,
we too would have summoned you to our reality
here in the secretless glare of sunlight,
bidden you select the prudent career,
embrace cautious choices;
would have had you marry,

replicate our worth with children,
watched your waist thicken and your hair pale,
responsibly, respectably,
resigned to the dulling of your eyes,
and left you at the end ungrudgingly,
content that you would tend our grave.

And for all our wisdom
would not have known
how idle was our hope, Anís,
who in that tearful hour
moping alone among the unaccusing dustmotes
in your shuttered room
conjured God's very face,
were pledged to lay your cheek's childbloom
upon His target breast,
your atoms elevated
to eternally commingle
with Dust of dust.

THE BLUNDER

Ṭihrán, 1852

Some blunder into history
by a simple act
without the panoply
of the punctilious marriage
that secures a dynasty,
without the calculatedly
outrageous flourish
or unconsidered heroic feat.

This nameless crone, for instance.
She purposefully hobbles
through the street's
loud and roiling crowd
toward her goal.
Care was never lavished
upon her face, teeth, hair;
she needed no cosmetic art
for her role
in this affair.

There is a magnificence
in her rage.
Stooped arthritically,
slowed by age,
yet she seizes up the stone,
strains to keep pace.
Swooning with imminence,
inebriate with righteousness,
she hurls the missile
toward the mark.
Indignation and triumph stain
the dignity of her punctate face.
Now we know
God accepts even intended virtue;
the gentle, clement target turns
to aid her blow.
Sluggish with its burden of finality
the stone describes a languid arc.

There in timeless tableau
we see Archetype and archetype:
but how to read its sense?
Does the hag know
she enacts our rejection
(who have not her innocence)?

CASE STUDY

As psychologists, gentlemen, you may wish to consider this study. By all means take notes.

The subjects are unexceptional in the context of the exceptional times. The youth, an only son, conventionally handsome and doted upon; the mother, simple and pious. In another period she would not likely have imagined a world more complex or demanding than her kitchen. What could be asked of one who has so little?

There were disturbances in Zanján, one might say, not to put too fine a point on it. The boy, then, handed over to the mob, is led to certain death. He has a noteworthy aplomb but countless youth have shown an equal valour in causes less than this. Rather, gentlemen, observe the mother, summoned to the place of execution. She strides impatiently toward this appointment so long foreseen. Familiar with giving, she had not thought to withhold this last token; gifts are given once and this was all decided long ago.

The enemy, relying heavily on the predictability of mothers, urges her to extend to her child the impertinent, the unforgivable invitation. Her life cannot purchase his nor her tears save him, so she rescues him from regret, sweetens his departure: *I will disown you as my son if you incline your heart to such evil whisperings and allow them to turn you away from the truth.*

The boy's choice condoned, he yields gladly to the sword. Dry-eyed with pride, approbation and knowledge of compensation, the mother sees the severed head roll toward her. She turns slowly from that sad souvenir—had never attached strings to her gifts nor asked receipt.

Well, gentlemen, there you have it; admittedly not a conventional domestic situation. Now, learned doctors, do you care to expatiate on sacrifice and resignation? Explain if you will, what is asked of us.

AT HER LOOKING GLASS

Ṭihrán
August 1852

No rings, then. I have almost done with symbols;
the white silk is enough.
The face a little flushed, I think—
          no colour needed there!
But even this becomes a willing bride. How eagerly
the blood goes to its task, and this but the beginning!

Ah, little mole that always troubled me, today
you are my jewel. Let me go to him flawed, human.
And oil of the rose—roses for love!—
for am I not a lover?

Yes, this will do. I like the spare economy of this;
this plainness pleases me.
Beauty (and they have said I have that) is best
achieved by discarding all but the essential.
          (Do you not see, my sons, the Bridge of Ṣiráṭ
          must be crossed alone?)
Is there an ode here?
          Ah well, no time for that. I have sung my songs
          and they succeed if they bring me this!

Yes, this will suffice—
        there is no room for vanity in this meeting,
        this appointment kept but once!
Let them hurry! Or does my unseemly haste
offend my beloved?
        My fast has made me giddy! How well
        he knows my joy!

Foolish woman! Would you forget the scarf?
        choose carefully now!—
yes, nuptial,
the finest,
softest,
and draped just so? Or carried?
        I kiss you, lovely thing, in anticipation
        of your sweet purpose!

Ah, how easy all this is.
Now let them come!
One more journey, one last garden.

        Soon, my unborn sisters,
        we shall see what comes of this!

HOW STILL THE CENTRE

    We are not astonished
    after the star-strewn career
    the drunkening drama
    the dark turbulence
    noisily tumbling her from periphery
    toward the wet sucking maw

of the angry vortex
to find
in the still and absolute centre
this bland and yawning domesticity:
    the woman pacing her room,
    sorting, arranging,
    consigning a few trinkets
    to a wooden chest
    for memento or bread-and-butter gift
and, as housewife to greengrocer,
milady to backstair maid,
issuing the calm order
    My last request
    is that you permit no one
    henceforth to enter my chamber . . .
in the confident excluding tone
born of the assured,
rare
and unsunderable marriage.

LULLABY

Are you infants that you will not sleep without my tales!
I swear you turn my poor head grey;
I have been far too soft with you.
If your mother knew we spoke like this
your poor old nurse would pay, my little tyrants.
Would you have your *nanú* disgraced that way?
Ah, but what harm—we are children only once
and that is brief enough.
Let me close the lattice against the laughter
from the banquet. The nightingales are still tonight.

So, you would have the story of the secret stone—
do you not tire of that old tale yet?
I fear to give you morbid dreams.
But yes, we all love secrets
and it satisfies me well to tell it;
I do not have an endless store, for all my years.

It was long ago, in Ṭihrán, in the time of your father's father,
cousin of the Kalántar.
I came as a young girl into the service of his wife.
My people were honest and my home decent.
I was clean in my ways, swift and soundless
on my feet and quick to learn.
Fate was often cruel in those harsh days
but I found a good life and pleased my mistress.
My hands could move gently as brown doves
across her silks, and I was skilful with the comb.

The day when one of high birth, a man of Núr,
was taken to the Síyáh-Chál, in chains,
the household was abuzz. A festival was made of it,
the servants watching from the roof
as he was led through the rabble of the streets.
I was glad enough of the event—not every day
one of my station can see a nobleman in such a plight,
and we had few entertainments.

A strange sight indeed—like seeing a white rose
in a swarm of gnats. He walked in dream-like majesty
as though he did not hear the curses and abuse—
his head bared, his feet unshod,
his garment soiled with refuse pelted by the mob.
In excitement I seized up a white pebble—sharp it was—
and raised my hand to hurl it.
And then he looked up at me, as though the better
to receive its full force.
I froze. It was his eyes, I think.

I turned and fled, sobbing and shaking.
Afterwards I was much teased by the others
for being an hysterical girl. In shame I hid the pebble.
And that was all.

Later he was exiled, I heard,
but what became of him I cannot say.
Some said he was an enemy of God,
and some a holy man.
I do not know about such things—
it was enough to have seen that face.
Perhaps I should have cast it, but my hand was stayed.
I took it as an omen.

I keep the stone in this small pouch about my throat—
you may touch it if you promise you will sleep—
see how smooth it is worn.
It grows, I think, more white each year.
The silly amulet of an old fool, I suppose,
but when I am ill or sad it comforts me.

Did I not close the window?
I smell the heavy breath of roses!

So there you have it; it was his eyes, you see.
It was as though they gazed beyond us to another world.

Now will you sleep, my little ones?

A DREAM OF FIRE

Mission of the Good Shepherd
Ṭihrán
15 September 1852

My dear Edwina,

It is not yet dawn and the house is still. I have wakened from a troubling dream and am too agitated to successfully court sleep. Therefore I have lighted a lamp, drawn a light shawl about my shoulders and taken up my pen to write to you. You will realize at once, my dearest sister, that I am shamelessly using you—I hasten to admit it at once—but the dream (about which I shall say more later) has left me not only sleepless but intensely homesick. For the first time since I so eagerly consented to accompany Aunt Edna on this adventure, begun now so many months ago, I am engulfed in homesickness—it is a keenly felt physical sensation, like waves of nausea, one might say, or the occasional distress one experiences on a sea voyage.

It must be that the night air and the stillness of the hour are conducive to confession—your intrepid, unorthodox little sister feels homesick! But with it I enjoy a delicious sensation of guilt and the small conceit in which I suppose all insomniacs indulge—the notion that I am the only one in the world awake at this hour. I picture you and Thomas as having long since retired to a deserved and blissful sleep, and the children folded into innocent dreams, their pink faces as sweet and mysterious as unopened blossoms. Your house in London I see as a warm refuge in the large impersonal city, a harbour from which sails forth in all weather the stable ship of the goodness of your lives whose cargo of genuine Christian charity and grace enriches all who enter the wake of your argosy. That last sentence, as I read it over, strikes me as being affected and preciously poetical—and in truth I have of late excessively exposed myself to the scant English library here in part no doubt to counteract the strangeness of this setting, to assuage my boredom and perhaps to cultivate and invite the homesickness I

97

am now experiencing in such full measure. But despite the extravagance of my flight of fancy I hope you will understand and accept the sincerity of my thought which I expressed, alas, so inadequately.

What I intended to say is that you and Thomas demonstrate your religious feelings so fully and naturally in your lives whereas for me, despite my struggle to achieve a sense of peace and to live a Christian life, faith of the quality I hope to acquire seems often an unattainable goal. I long to have been able to inherit faith, as you have, with an unquestioning humility and gratitude (and must now, I see, add envy to my growing list of sins!) The minor mortifications of the flesh I impose upon myself (such as not spending *quite* as much time at my toilet as my vanity invites me to) do not bring spiritual attainment but do, I hope, serve to ward off apathy and self-satisfaction. In my darkest moments my Spirit chafes against my desire to believe and to experience the reality of religious truth; indeed I sometimes feel that whatever degree of faith I have is of no more consequence to my soul than a mosquito bite to my physical body. Perhaps, I tell myself, I have only willed myself to believe. In you and Thomas I do not see such a conflict—you wear your beliefs as comfortably and unselfconsciously as you do your skin. Will I ever achieve that wonderful condition? It saddens me unbearably to imagine I might not.

I know you would attempt to console me at this moment by making kind allusions to my serving as companion to Aunt Edna on her visit to Cousin Robert's Mission and my willingness to serve here temporarily as a nurse but I must perforce dismiss your charitable observation at once, it being swept away before the cold onrushing recognition that I was prompted in this instance, as in so many others, not by a desire to serve our Lord but by a crasser motive—my vile curiosity and selfish wish to see foreign lands. An even more difficult admission is that the dreadful sin of vanity played no small part in my making this journey—my vain hope of proving to myself that I am the epic woman I thought myself to be when I was a child—and the perhaps equally sterile hope of meeting the challenge of some great and mysterious destiny.

I suppose—no, I must say I know, for I try to be honest with myself (at least in important matters!)—I know that I have set aside the question of marriage until some of my questions are answered. Surely marriage is not the highest destiny of a woman! Oh dearest, I do not mean to hurt you for I have nothing but the deepest love and admiration for you and Thomas and I believe with all my heart that you perfectly fulfil God's purpose in your family life—I mean only that I have not been able yet to find established in myself the sure foundation of belief you have achieved on which a family and home, in the fullest sense of those words, must rest. Mama always complained of my wilful and headstrong ways and I am sure she is convinced that I have barred myself from the Garden of Eden (she so *clearly* sees marriage in that light) and have dealt unfairly with Stephen. What is important to me is that I have never lied to him. I have resisted his suit with a cool aloofness, although I admire him very much, and it delights me on the one hand that he should endeavour so earnestly to understand, and on the other it vexes me to distraction that he should consent as he did to await my return from here to give him my final answer. My heart and head continue their battle for domination of me! Do not think that I shall never marry—I may yet marry Stephen—for I long for a home and children but these things must be, for me, a part of a more imperative destiny, if only I may find it.

Will you chide me for pouring out these rambling thoughts in this letter rather than confiding them blushingly to my journal as well-bred romantic young ladies are expected to? The truth of the matter is that my diary has remained untouched for days and I cannot bring myself to write a line. Recently I glanced over the entries and they seemed to me to be of excruciating triteness. I had thought the record I proposed to keep would be the means of my entertaining you and Thomas and the children with exciting tales when we gathered around the fire after tea upon my return to England (it would be raining outside, of course, and we would be a cosy warm circle near the hearth) but I find the words flat and dull and perhaps not even true. Since the journal does not interest me I cannot imagine that it will be a source of interest to anyone else, no matter how dear they hold me in affection. I was bored by my tedious descriptions of our voyage, my enthusiastic account of the strange sounds and sights and scents of Persia, the trivial details of life at the Mission and the dull recounting of our side trips to centres outside Ṭihrán and what we saw and ate and whom we met and what we said, my superficial and probably inaccurate dissertations on the subtle mind of the Oriental and the morals and manners of the Persians—none of it now strikes me as being of any significance. It is all so banal, like those countless journals I have read by travellers in Europe which I seized up so eagerly because they held out so much hope of answering the need of the soul but which contained, after all, nothing but descriptions of mountains. I do not feel *myself* when I write in my journal—who am I addressing when I write in it?—and because it intimidates me I become formal and conventional like a school girl composing a 'correct' letter to Mama. I am dissatisfied, too, with the water-colour sketches I have made here; they are pallid and smugly proper and cannot possibly convey what I have seen or experienced in this curious country.

Instead, I think what may be of more lasting interest are my letters. I hope you have kept them. It occurs to me that I shall enjoy reading them again some day. They constitute, I daresay, a more honest record of my journey—I almost wrote 'quest' and I do not dispute the accuracy of the impulse that led me to that substitution. Perhaps if I read my letters at a later time I shall find some key in them to what I have searched for all my life; perhaps my own destiny is written into them in some cryptogrammic fashion as yet indecipherable and veiled from me.

Alas, another flight of fancy! You will be impatient with my musing in this aimless way. To aid you in your ever-forthcoming forgiveness of me, reflect on the fact that I have changed so little since you last saw me—always consulting the tea leaves and the Tarot, tearing apart the flower to find its invisible heart, searching for the unknowable secret of existence. Do you remember how I would waken in the morning as a child bitterly sobbing because I could not remember the beauty and mystery of some dream that had been interrupted by sunlight flooding the room or by nanny's call? I was always certain that the meaning would have been revealed if I had not been disturbed.

I have said little in my previous letters about Cousin Robert but it is a comfort to speak of him now under cover of secret darkness for I am troubled by what I see. Although I saw him but infrequently at home and knew him not well I find him strangely changed and cannot believe he finds that life here has met his expectations. He is a saddened, disillusioned and almost embittered man. If Aunt Edna has observed this she has not revealed her thoughts to me nor is she likely to do so. As many rigid people do she demands propriety in life rather than happiness. I sense in Cousin Robert no joy but instead a kind of grim obstinacy, and feel that he remains here through some personal need of his own. I can even imagine myself adopting a similar attitude of resignation if I were to remain here long. He truly needs our prayers! And privately I pray that I either find a living faith and joyful conviction or else lose faith altogether, for I should not want religion to become for me a spiritless habit or a formula clung to through loyalty or fear. Forgive me, dearest, if I seem to stand in judgement; we may be sure that God well knows what is in Cousin Robert's heart and blesses his service. I simply wish he were happier than he appears to be and long to know what he really feels about God and faith. We cannot speak together of these matters because he treats me rather patronizingly, perhaps to conceal from me the weight of his failure, and he firmly assigns me the role of 'visiting distant relative'. Even his many kindnesses seem designed to create distance between us. (How *uncharitable* of me! But it does seem so. There is, in all the kind things he does, the laboured and elaborate quality

of one who does not like children extending himself for a child
out of a sense of form or duty.)

No doubt there are reasons for all this. As I told
you in an earlier letter this is not a fertile field for Mission
work. The Muslims are incurious and indifferent to the Christian message and pick their way among the various Missions
as disinterestedly as they do among the competing stalls in the
bazaar, whilst the Jews view us with an ill-concealed hostility.
How strange we must seem to both groups, divided as we are in
our own faith! I am able to sympathize in some degree with
what is, I suspect, the amused disgust with which even those
who pose as friends or converts view us.

Cousin Robert's friends—if they may be so designated—are for the most part associated with other Missions,
vague and dispirited people who hold each other in tepid
esteem through sheer loneliness. European, British and
American, Christians of all persuasions are united in an un-
affectionate, formal and uneasy fashion through a shared contempt of the barbarous Orientals, and most of our social
engagements are given over to their despairing accounts of
Persian intractability, deviousness and unredeemable savagery. I have grown so weary of it I could scream! And even
these dismal gatherings have been curtailed in recent weeks
due to the unrest that is sweeping some areas of the country
because of the activities of the Bábí movement about which
I wrote to you.

A veritable holocaust of fury has been unleashed
against them by the Muslims. The reports of the indecent and
gruesome tortures and the ferocious slaughter of which they
are the victims are so heinous that they cannot bear repeating.
I cannot sift through the conflicting accounts of their doctrines
to determine what it is they believe or why they should be the
object of such furious attacks. They include in their number
men of important standing, great lords, members of the clergy,
military men and merchants; and the Muslim community is
seething with rumours and accounts blaming or approving the
Bábís, exalting them or heaping upon them maledictions and

the vilest curses. The view generally held among Cousin Robert's friends is that they are heretical and politically dangerous. It is said the Bábís—men, women and even *children!*—go to their deaths bravely, chanting the praises of God and singing hymns. What a strange and powerful vision must inspire or delude them. I confess I am both intrigued and horrified and in a curious way envious—Oh! to be able to *believe* so deeply in anything! And yet I recoil from the idea, unlikely though it is, of such an uncontrollable force as animates the Bábís overleaping the borders of this country and sweeping Europe and the rest of the world into a maelstrom of chaos. I would hope in such event to shield you and Thomas and the children from it with my own body if need be; I could easily die to protect and secure the virtue and tranquillity of your good lives. No doubt the ferment here will gradually dissipate, though one of Cousin Robert's friends remarked that it is certain the martyrdom of the Bábís will win them new adherents and admirers and that it is great unwisdom on the part of the authorities not to let the movement die for lack of momentum.

In my earlier letters and perhaps at wearisome length I have raged and railed against the plight of women in this country. I was deeply stirred to learn that among those who in past weeks were caught up in the turmoil surrounding the Bábís was a woman named Qurratu'l-'Ayn who, I am told, was one of outstanding beauty and intelligence and a poet of considerable merit. She was put to death in a most horrible fashion, strangled with her own scarf. She seems by all accounts a most unusual figure to emerge in this land—the women I have met are vapid, fatuous and bovine—and one would least expect a woman of her calibre to be affected by this movement unless she saw herself as a suffragist or was a visionary like Ste Jeanne d'Arc. Already she is something of a legend among the Muslims. I am desperate to know more about her—the information which reaches us is so garbled and sparse (and, I may say, coloured by the bias and contempt of the narrator) that one cannot ever be sure one has possession of the facts or understood them. My interest in the Bábí movement seems somewhat to embarrass Cousin Robert and his associates and more than once they have furtively interrupted their conversation when I entered the room. It is almost as though they were jealous of the rapidity of growth of the Bábí movement measured against the scant fruit of their own sincere, often sacrificial but seemingly unrewarded efforts. The massacre of the Bábís seems of interest to them only as an illustration (rather welcomed!) of the innate and insatiable savagery of the Oriental nature.

It is likely that these unsettling events gave rise to the dream from which I arose tonight trembling and excited beyond recall of sleep. I shall tell you what I remember of it for I shall be interested in reading this record when I return to London and have long since forgotten the details. As is often the case I seemed both to witness the dream and participate in it and I remember that I saw colours. I stood, it seemed, on a high mountain at the utmost tip of the earth, or perhaps even was suspended above it for I could see the globe below me, the mountains and oceans clearly defined. Before me stood a woman—in the dream I did not question but that it was Qurratu'l-'Ayn—clad in a dazzling white gown and a veil of the kind worn by Eastern women. I was wearing my ordinary clothes—my garnet muslin, in fact, for I remember thinking how dull the fabric looked compared with her gown—and I, too, was veiled in the fashion of women here in some grey diaphanous stuff. The woman gazed at me in silence and with great intensity as though probing my soul. She then drew from behind her a small book exquisitely illuminated in Oriental motif and with a resolute and deliberate movement removed her veil. As she cast her eyes upon the book's open pages the little volume burst into brilliant flames. I knew, as one does in dreams, that it was the book of life and that it held the answer to my heart's deepest question and I was overcome with a longing to read it. As I approached to do so the woman again looked into my eyes. With a solemn deliberation she touched the book to the hem of her lovely robe and then, as she placed the book in my hand, she became a column of gold flame. It was flame without heat or smoke—like the fire in the heart of a jewel—and it gave forth a wonderful fragrance. There was no horror in any of this—it seemed a most natural event though I was shaking with excitement.

I looked upon the book's pages and could see nothing but the brilliant fire and knew I must remove my veil. It would not yield! I tore at it firmly and then with frenzy, my heart bursting with anguish. Dropping the book I clawed frantically at the thin obscuring gauze, screaming aloud in vexation and awoke hearing the echo of my own cry to find my fingers beating the air and my face wet with tears. It was so vivid that I shiver to remember it!

And so I began this letter in a mood of desolate deprivation and homesickness in the dark hours and see now through the window that the sky has lightened and the pale stars of morning mock my foolishness. It will be another warm day. Life stirs here at an early hour. The gardener in the courtyard below is moving about raw with sleep and is indolently fussing about the tuberoses. He is a slow-moving man, mean in spirit, and has, I think, no love of flowers; but Cousin Robert tolerates or is indifferent to him.

The spell of homesickness has not yet fully left me but it will give way to the trivial routine of the day. Soon I must prepare Aunt Edna's tea and coddled egg; she does not entrust so delicate an undertaking to the staff. No doubt she would ask this of me even if we were guests in the palace of the Sháh. I think she feels that the English invented tea and the coddled egg!

I neglected to tell you that Aunt Edna's lettter of introduction to Lt-Col Justin Sheil has resulted in our being invited to tea next week. I understand that his wife is charming and attractive and I eagerly look forward to meeting her. She has, I am informed, followed the Bábí movement with considerable interest and is thought to be well informed. Perhaps she can satisfy my curiosity or throw some light on the confused and conflicting reports that have come to us. If anything interesting comes of it I shall write in detail, you may be sure. I plan to wear a wonderful turquoise silk you have not seen— you cannot imagine the beauty of the silk here.

Greet Thomas with deep affection and kiss the children for me. May God keep you well and in good spirits until we are reunited.

I remain your ever-devoted and loving sister,

Veronica

THE SALT

Tell us, young man, outstretched upon the rack,
Is hot brand on your soft flesh felt as kiss,
And butcher's cruellest blow a lover's act,
His searing touch a source of rapturous bliss?
Speak to us, lad, of pure love's highest use—
(Pain, cherished bride to whom your hands uplift?)
Do you translate as song the foe's abuse
And vilest gesture welcome as a gift?
What school, unruly boy, did you attend
And what diploma win to qualify
As rare salt of the Tablets of the Friend—
You, truly crowned, as those who never die?

Tell, tell, Bádí', before fiend stills your tongue,
Is rashness virtue only in the young?

RUBÁBIH

Yazd, 1903

This bed-wise woman
has known too many men,
lives beyond expectation of kindness
in a sad knowledge
unameliorated by surprise.

Interrupting a yawn
she now moves to her window,
watches impassively
the man dragged through the street;
sees the mob wrest from his body
his sobbing, clinging wife
who is beaten unconscious,
left torn and bleeding,
obscenely exposed,
as the perverse procession moves on.
In the hushed sector
the shutters close indifferently
on the still form
of the wounded woman
and her whimpering children.
Not even the prurient
or idly curious
remain in the deserted street.
Rubábih, who knows the world
to be this way,
sighs heavily at recognition
of yet another variation
of rejection.

Even stereotypes make choices.
Let's not be astonished
that it is she who descends,

gathers the children,
carries the victim on her back
to house and heal her:
Outcasts, one remembers,
have nothing to lose;
have, in every age,
come highly recommended.

PART FOUR:

SONGS AND SONNETS

A tender tumult stirs meek dust to motion,
A green and gentle violence weights each bough,
Strained the net wouldst banquet from this ocean;
Another song, another season now.

Roger White

LINES FROM A BATTLEFIELD

Ponder awhile. Hast thou ever heard that friend and foe
should abide in one heart? Cast out then the stranger, that
the Friend may enter His home.

Bahá'u'lláh

Come, let me fête you, beloved foe,
for I tire of this old-born war.
It would shorten did I not so ruinously adore
each endearing stratagem your consummate cunning devises;
your enamouring intransigence enchants me,
your very implacability an aphrodisiac.
In this moment when fatigue calls truce
let me say it: if I loved you less
I should not plot your end
as we embrace.
Clasped to your bosom I gauge it for my blade's dark use.
Beware the honey posset and my proffered kiss!
Caressing your unloosed hair I plait a noose
and with a traitor's hand I stroke your face.
May it be said I loved my enemy
but sought the Friend.

In these graceless hours
when faith strains feebly against the unbelieving night
I am alienated from angels and celestial concerns,
unmoved by the testimony of flowers.
Locked in a grief so ancient as to have no name,
in this dimming light,
even magnificence menaces, estranging me from excellence,
trivializing my pitiable trophies—minor virtues garnered
in a sweeter time—
my nurtured imperfections not so epically egregious
as to embarrass the seraphim ruefully yawning
at their mention;
nor will my shame, as once I thought,
topple the cities, arrest the sun's climb.

What assault on heaven guarantees attention?
Inured to the banality of pain
and the ordinariness of suffering (sanctified or plain!)
it is joy that is remembered.

Ah well, not every day can witness an anabasis
and I, a sorry soldier, camp in ruins,
speak from weariness of battle far prolonged.
From shining names on scattered tombs
I fashion a paean; to vanquish dread, invoke the victors:
        Breakwell/Brittingham/Blomfield/Benke/Bolles/Baker
        Barney/Bailey/Backwell/Bourgeois/Bosch
(Do I presume?
I swear a radiant rank appears,
assuring as sunlight,
familiar as bread!)
        Dunn/Dole/Dodge
        sterling Esslemont! rare Wilhelm!
        unrivalled Townshend of the silver pen!
        imbiber of the scarlet cup, Badí'!
        shield of the Cause, Samandarí!
        brilliant Keith! immortal Lua! steadfast Thornton!
        courageous Marion! incomparable Martha!
        constant Juliet!
        noble Louis of the golden heart!
        selfless Sutherland!
        Duarte Vieira, ebony prince!
        Johanna Schubarth!
Conquerors of continents, movers of hearts,
they are a legion stretching to horizon's end,
champions of the Peerless,
the darlings of the Friend.

A beachhead beckons. I read auguries of triumph
in my campfire's dwindling plumes.
Remove the garland, still the lyre, my love.
It is dawn: the engagement resumes.

IN THE SILENT SHRINE AN ANT

It behoveth the people of Bahá to die to the world and all
that is therein . . .

Bahá'u'lláh

In this sovereign and articulate silence
Will faith seize the dull, recalcitrant heart,
Beat down the truculent will and cleanly part
The passionate mind from violence,
The stratagems and dogma of our curtained lives?
We court a miracle and see the candles fail,
The petals rust. What do our tears avail?

No sword of vengeance cleaves us as we stand,
Our supplication brings no answering shout.
An ant crawls by persistent as our doubt
And in the comprehending hush we understand
Our mediocrity and godliness:
We are the question and its own reply.
The heartbeat thunders: Here, Lord, here am I!

But stillness gives us back with scented breath,
Who chooses love of Me must first choose death.

WHO HAD NO CANDLE

He Who had no candle
has here, ensconced in circled circle,
amid adoring flowers
and green deferential trees,
this whitest marble taper
tipped with gold.
It gleams serenely from Carmel,
inextinguishably lights the world,

our reverential hearts
the willing wick.

This light will melt
remotest snows,
outlast the names
by which we know it.

See, Ádhirbáyján,
this constant flame
which casts no shadow.

ASK IN PERSEPOLIS

Why should we honour these who spurned our world,
Our exhortations, prizes and our praise,
Turned their back on prudence, reason's pearl,
And solid, vital commerce of our days?

> *Persepolis, tell out your tale:*
> *What shall fade and what prevail?*

Why should we honour these who held no hope
For our fastidious scholarship, our power;
Who sought a kingdom past our mortal scope,
Held cheap the fleetness of man's salient hour?

> *Ask crumbling Grecian marble bust:*
> *What shall endure and what leave dust?*

Why should we honour these who held the earth
As less than pebble sinking in the mire?
We gladly would have tutored them in worth,
Shown all to which deserving men aspire.

> *Ask slave in market-place of Rome:*
> *Who leaves trace, who tomb and bone?*

Why should we honour these who scorned our gold,
Dismissed as insignificant our dream?
In future times our history will be told,
Theirs be erased as written on a stream.

> *Ask in Chile, Chad and Khmer:*
> *Does life but lead to sepulchre?*

Why should we honour these of no acclaim
Who followed vapoury image as thing real;
Who found flamboyant deaths and left no name,
Proved deaf to cogent logic's stern appeal?

> *Ask the wise ones of Tabríz:*
> *Did darkened sun at noon bring ease?*

Our lofty errands could not stay their course,
Nor woman, wine nor wisdom cause to veer;
Perversely doomed, accursed by evil source,
They turned from all the beautiful and dear.

> *Stones of 'Akká, be our eyes:*
> *On what Beauty does sun rise?*

We shall not honour these who did not see
The scheme our cautious wisdom would apply,
The ordering of the world our destiny
And theirs, who follow phantoms, but to die.

> *Ask on earth, ask in heaven:*
> *Which the loaf, which the leaven?*

Then leave the world to us, who steer by star
Anciently fixed by will and intellect;
We design the wars and spires, course afar,
Posterity inherits the effect.

> *Historian, pray judge it well:*
> *what path heaven, what path hell?*

NEW SONG

And he hath put a new song in my mouth . . .

Psalms 40:3

It was comfortable in the smalltown smugness
of your childhood.
You were born securely into salvation's complacent trinity,
a Catholic, Protestant or Jew.
In a spasm of spiritual megalomania
you praised His good judgement in selecting
such eminently deserving souls
for the gift of His exclusive One True Faith.
But only on Sundays.
The world was small and safe and familiar.
And very white.
No red or black offended
our prim steepled vaults of self- congratulation.
Indians were the bad guys who got licked in movies,
dying copiously amid candy wrappers
and the popcorn smell of matinees.
Amos and Andy probably lived in some far place,
like Hollywood,
or maybe in the radio. And there was no proof
that God spoke Negro.
You knew that He loved Canadians—they didn't start wars.
He would approve our thrift and industry
and seeing our virtuous sunlit wheatfields,
our unpretentious brick,
He would agree with the Chamber of Commerce
that ours was a good town in which to live.
Yes, it was comfortable then.

Of course there were a handful who found solace
in the medicinal doctrines of Muriel Sweetbun Udder,
or the burnished tablets of Myron J. Hammerschmitt;
a few who gathered in tents or behind vacant storefronts with

ambitious titles attesting orthodoxy or reformation;
but then every town has its malcontents.
A small brave band scorned our comicbook catechism,
our insolent litany of insularity,
and made a kind of faith of not-believing.
Still, God did not strike them dead.
He was said to be extraordinarily patient
with sinners and heathens.
When you heard that God had died, you wondered
whether it was from sheer boredom—
all that joyless music and our impudent prayers.
Your sophomoric selfrighteousness would have been enough
to do Him in.

So you would have described it then,
the frightened child
striving against acne and Auschwitz
and an anger that sought release in a word powerful enough
to shake the universe,
intimidate the stars,
blind to His love of the people of your town
for the innocence of their aspiration;
blind to their genuine virtue and power and beauty.

The tempest came in your twelfth or fifteenth year,
a clean cold wind,
and you were left like a stripped young tree in autumn
with a cynical winter setting in
and nothing large enough to house your impulse to believe.
The need lay as quiet, unhurried and insidious as a seed
snowlocked in a bleak and lonely landscape.
But forgiveness came, an unselective flooding rain,
and the seed was there, a promise kept.
Even your rejection was forgiven
and, in the burgeoning, lovesap slowly stirred.
God hadn't died, of course, abandoned us for Russia,
nor moved to Uganda.

You caught a glimpse of Him in the clearing smoke of the rifles
in the barrack-square of Tabríz;
heard a whisper in the soft silk dress of Ṭáhirih, bridally white.
His fragrance was carried by the wind startling the wildflowers
of the fields of Bárfurús͟h where Quddús was felled.
The stones of 'Akká saw His beauty and His pain
and cried aloud.
On Carmel's sandy slope you traced the outline of His tent
and saw, in its tall cypress,
the talisman of His triumph.

There is a new song.
Up from the Síyáh-C͟hál it rose, breaking the S͟háh's dream;
the Sultán turned in terror as its sweetness grew.
It echoed through the palaces of Europe, empty now.
The bells grew silent, the minarets fell mute;
the full-risen sun embarrassed our disputatious sputtering
candles. Our doomed and desperate dissonance was stilled,
trickling out like the dismal incense
rising from our saddened, separate altars.
The dust of S͟híráz throbbed as Thornton Chase took up the
song and all the roses of Írán
spilled their musk triumphantly at Lua's peal.
Martha heard the music; its accents captivated May.
Westward it moved, and worldward,
rejoicing the trees of Adrianople as the chorus grew—
                    Esslemont, Breakwell, Dreyfus—
and grew
and grew.
Now the earth is flooded with the felicity of this new song,
this Godsong.

I falter, Lord,
I quaver;
yet I sing.

SONNETS FOR THE FRIEND

I

To whom am I to sing if not to You
Who know, well know, the singer and the season
And listen still and know the verse be true
Who are Himself the music and its reason.
My barren fields lie parched beneath the sun
Nor orange and olive yield in arid earth
And fallow stay till husbanded by One
Whose pledge embodies all of death and birth.
Of what then shall I sing if not of this:
I learn the ancient patience of the land,
Mute witness to misfortune's scorching kiss
And reach for rain, as reached I for Your hand.
When I but sound Your name in prayer or dream
Behold! My rivers run, my orchards teem.

II

Why would You have my feeble, feckless love?
Another's charm compellingly holds sway.
Inconstant, from Your kiss I'd turn away
Often and often to him, the mated dove
Truer than I, more passionately whole.
I share another's wine-cup and embrace.
Encouched with You, I'd helplessly extol
The enslaving power of that other's grace.
Your song would not hold me. With half my heart
I'd hear You and at faintest first call flee
Truckling and grovelling to my sweet, tart
And jealous love who asks fidelity.
Yet, faithfully, You call this faithless one
And stumbling, halt, at last to You I run.

What love exacts I had not thought to yield,
Nor guessed the crazing dart the Hunter hurled,
Or might have found indifference a shield
And built of gold and pride a dullard's world.
But sure the Marksman's aim and keen His sight;
I could but dress His raven locks the night.
I might have fled His perfumed, silken tent
But for the madding blandishment of grape;
Heart ravished by His voice, resistance rent
And, flagon drained, I could not seek escape.
In passion's sweeping tide I lost all fear
And could but stroke my Captor's brow the year.
What love demands I had not thought to give
Who, dead of this, am yet left here to live.

A METROPOLIS OF OWLS

*... It was not the Black Dungeon of Ṭihrán, for all its
horrors and chains, which He (Bahá'u'lláh) named the
Most Great Prison. He gave that name to 'Akká. ...
Not He Himself alone but the Cause of God was in prison.*

George Townshend

Named by her past suitors 'Akká, Ptolemais, St Jean d'Acre,
she is no beauty, this aged courtesan, meanly rouged by sun,
squalidly abandoned to beg her bread
with perversely tasteless baubles
and tawdry bits of tarnished brass,
her historically frequented bed
the nest of roach and rodent.

The moon's cosmetic kindness does not erase
the horror-hollowed haggardness of her pocked, stone face.
The enthusiastic stars fail to cajole
nor can the soaring birdsong raise in her joyless breast
an answering trill.
The wafting apotropaic perfume of the Bahjí rose,
seeking to condole,
pleads for entry at her unrelenting gate, but is turned back,
its forgiveness spent
among children playing on Napoleon's Hill.

With disconsolate dusk the carnival of her bazaar subsides
leaving her in darkness, with no warming fire,
leaning toward the water's edge
where the mortified day will expire.
Low-squatting, knees clasped to her thin unsuccouring chest,
she does not raise her bat-encircled head
at the hawk's cry,
nor heed the querulous questions of the owl.
The pale paste jewel of her lighthouse beckons wanly
but the senile, impotent mosque can only lewdly smile.
She does not see the stricken night huddling comfortlessly
by her garment's soiled, unfastened hem
nor hear her own demented keening echoed in the lamenting
surf's low moan,
much less gaze adoringly at Carmel entreating greenly
from across the bay.
Indifferent to the lascivious mist
obscenely fingering her lank hair
her stare is inward,
fixed upon her private stunning grief,
turned from the world,
consumed beyond self-pity or contrition.

She knows the moment when she chose her death,
knows it, lives it, nightly
as the murmurous sin-whispering waves pile in,

forty upon forty,
restless with accusation:
    the Cargo of cargoes ignominiously spewed ashore;
    the metallic futile protest of the rusted chain;
    the thickening indignation of the sordid, misled mob;
    the unwilling lock-key turning in a prison cell;
    the infamous *farmán* piously read (she knows it well,
        the parchment crackling wildly in her reeling brain);
    the shattered skylight and the frail youth's twisted frame;
    the mother's sob
    and then
    and then
        Oh then, unbearably, the scratching of a Pen!

The dawn releases her to trinkets, plastic wares,
the haggling of housewives,
and leering merchants' trivial affairs.

She rises shivering, and disfiguring her face,
rehearses a grotesque, coquettish smile
for her reeking market-place;
but leaving, looks back to where
the denunciatory waves recede,
her unspeakable, lip-locked, bosom-buried crime
(till their eve's retelling)
a secret aqueously kept:
    To have seen the loneliness of God
    and not have wept!

ALWAYS IT IS WOMEN

It is women, always women, who reveal the way,
who see and understand what well serves life.
Forced from prehistoric day
to yield in love and birth,
to bend and stoop to cradle, fire and field
they gazed to earth
were befriended by what nurtures
and grew wise.

Men went gladly whooping to the hunt
happy with the power to devise
schemes of war, instruments of death
and magic to hold congress with the stars.
If the rich game thinned or weather turned adverse
they might placate capricious spirits,
blame illest luck or totem's curse
and range afar. But women knew.
Leaning and listening they learned
what in stillness is acutely earned.
Crouched closest to the soil
they saw the berry sicken,
the water fail,
the sweet clay spoil,
knew incantation would not avail
nor sacrifice behoove.
Soon the camp would move.

It was the Magdalene who as she pored
over the dust that held her Lord
read the message of the Nazarene
and knew for what the men must cast their nets.
Always it is women who reveal the way
and who, conceiving, conceive what fosters life.
But man forgets.

Again it is a woman.
At Ba<u>sh</u>t, prostrate in prayer,
she hears the shrilling trumpet pierce the air
and knows the Nightingale is listening.
Rising she tears off her veil,
steps blazing, glistening, from her tent—
the past is rent.
Men groan in consternation,
constellations pale,
the age shudders, reels and dies.

Slowly the camp moves toward
the world that she espies.

THE CAPTIVE

*There was one name that always brought joy to the face of
Bahá'u'lláh. His expression would change at the mention
of it. That name was Mary of Magdala.*

'Abdu'l-Bahá

I

You, Mary of Magdala,
there in your garden of pleasure,
amid the jasmine and the sweet, green figs,
going your perfumed way,
secure in your Roman's love,
knowing the ways of men,
    but waiting, waiting;
your dreams cool as your pavilion's marbled floor,
contained, guarded,

blanched and rustling like the gnarled olive,
your heart testing the coils of love,
remembering your village home,
  your heart captive, captive.

II

You, scented and oiled,
your glistening hair a dark cascade,
smooth-armed, gold-bangled,
fingers slender, turquoise-laden,
stroking the ivoried lute,
your smile dawning, tentative in trust,
or flashing and accomplished in guile,
often alone,
  waiting, waiting,
or, not alone,
practised in words men wish to hear;
sometimes weary of the songs, the wine, the dice,
all games of chance;
and sometimes sad,
your thoughts an echo of the mourning dove,
pensive, bleating,
alone in a world of men,
  your mind captive, captive.

III

You, marking one man,
unlike, apart,
one beyond your art, your wiles,
one knowing, accepting as none has,
true as sunlight,
one to warm the marble dream,
to still the dry and rustling tree,
to hush the dove's lament,
one who is for ever,
his words a soft rain on that stony hill,

you, listening, listening,
starting in anguish at the augury
of the red anemone
there on the sanded slope
parched in the slanting sun.

IV

You, learning one kind of death,
seeing your Roman go, go baffled,
bronzed and glinting in the sun's last rays,
go to his legion and to other loves,
go in anger, jealous, proud,
not knowing how, alone in the chilled and darkened villa,
you fill the lilac dusk with sobs;
and he, wondering, wondering,
why you should will him go,
why his wealth nor power not hold you,
and why his gods have failed.

V

You, in simple robes,
coarse against the pampered flesh,
following the other
the long miles through the dust,
with the faithful women and the few and urgent men,
unmindful of discomfort,
your peasant source remembered,
his smile your nectar,
his word your bread,
thrall to his will,
    learning, learning,
giving alms,
growing in grace,
resuming humble ways,
    your will captive, captive.

VI

You, with fragrant spices,
lavishing unschooled kisses
on the unshod feet,
your tears their true anointment;
and are not done with weeping
but will kiss that head
that bears the bitter garland
hanging above you on yet another barren hill,
    you, waiting, waiting,
while love dims and ebbs
and the world goes on, uncaring.

VII

You, seeing the voiceless vault
and seeing more, oh more,
the light dazzling, dazzling,
the hurt dissolving in the balm;
then hastening, hastening
to tell the gentle, grieving friends,
you, radiant with seeing,
the first to know, to see.

VIII

You, now brimming with the vision,
ignited, a gladdener of ears,
telling of love's kingdom,
lip to lip, town to town,
making many journeys,
    calling, calling,
breast to breast, land to land.
An Emperor will hear you—but stone, but stone.
Only jaded Rome,
darkening, doomed and sinking,

will still your voice;
but none will still your song.
Others call: the spires of Europe will rise.

IX

And you, Mary of Magdala, dying for him at the end,
triumphantly dying,
rejoicing in this death,
your Roman looking on,
        puzzling, puzzling,
who still would save you
had you not abandoned all love's lesser claims
and are dying, dying,
ecstatic in this death for love,
        your soul captive, captive.
You, Mary of Magdala,
so magnificent your thraldom
that down the centuries
at sounding of your name,
Love Incarnate,
God's Own Thrall,
smiles.

SUPPLIANT: BAHJÍ

Is this then all there is, a simple garden,
And a silence that displaces need for words?
What portent in the blood-red wayside poppy?
What message in the music of the birds?

The hero's heart is hoisted on a cypress,
The saint's is softly folded as a rose;
But mine lies shattered here among the pebbles
On the only path the fainting coward knows.

RAINY EVENINGS IN GREAT CITIES

Always
on rainy evenings
in great cities
when I am passing on a bus
I see
beneath a brightly lit marquee
a slender girl
clasping a pathetically inadequate umbrella
a rippling crowd
floating about her
on a crest of animated chatter
on which they glide
out of the black
through the submarine light
into the theatre
swirling to either side
in twos and threes
gregariously grouped, companionably coupled,
selected, grown insolent,
she parting them like an apologetic boulder
her hair a little damp
forehead glistening with rain or stigmata
face pale and straining.
I watch her pantomime of anticipation
as she consults her watch
with unnecessary frequency
establishing credence, purpose,
her eyes eagerly scanning the faces
lips, lifting, parting
in what would be for him
a familiar smile
if he existed.
The cruel light exposes her unanswerable loneliness
as if by X-ray.

Always I wonder
how she can be seen
on rainy evenings
in each great city
when I pass on a bus
and how I know
that she will see the play or film alone.
Inexorably my bus moves on
a mindless mastodon
to an unknown destination
and the windows look on darkness.
Her picture stays with me forever
a slide arrested in projection.
Overhead the bus ads pitilessly postulate
that loneliness is cured by choice of toothpaste.
It is the girl's umbrella that enrages me:
Never has it shielded her from disappointment.

SONGS OF SEPARATION

Are you interested in renunciation?
'Abdu'l-Bahá

I

Love would suffice me, I'd have bade it stay,
And sinned, if this it be, implored our God
In mercy cast His eyes another way
To win my will, and not have thought it odd.
But you who are much less than I a fool
Knew rootless tree could not survive the frost
And, leaving, drank renunciation's gruel,
So loved me as to pay the torn heart's cost.

Though blade to breast would be an easier death
And meagre comfort's found in sage advice,
Though separation tortures with each breath
And roses in my hands now turn to ice,
Yet what you dared foresee I've come to know:
I claim you still because I let you go.

II

Our love will pass unnoticed into time
And history not record our names or cause,
Nor future lovers weep to read this rhyme,
The hastening crowd not give it thought or pause;
Yet must I write these lines for my heart's ease,
Recall our perfect hour, taste again
The wine pressed from a berried moment seized,
Joy's lavish-yield—even, yes, the pain.
Had I but known that exile were the toll
Still would I offer that committed kiss,
Release you then to God for His Own role
Though death itself were paler deed than this.
In banishment, I learn that this is true:
I gave Him all, thus gives He ever you.

III

I hold you in my mind and think of death
As ever it was lover's wont to do,
Would barter every spoil, my very breath,
To be empowered to stay that hand from you.
Were our devotion but the only stake
I might betray it for a lesser prize;
With heaven ours, the covenant we make
Exalts our trust beyond all compromise.
Love outgrown proof, it now remains to find
Acceptance of our parting for the feast;
Our final fear, when this to one assigned,
Survivor be endowed to bear it least.

Host chooses guest, yet does this coward pray
Soul's strengthening, lest he be bidden stay.

<h2 style="text-align:center">IV</h2>

Would that the times were tame and lovers free
To savour life's most brief and scented hours
Oblivious of history, besieged towers,
The chaos and the unmoored stars; but we
Are wrenched, torn, flung as unremembered leaves
Driven in doleful patterns the wind weaves.
Glad days are gone. A bastion given each
The long nightwatch begins. From fitful dreams
I waken wet-lashed, racked by choking screams,
Seeing you fall, alone, beyond the reach
Of my caress and comfort, dying there—
Your lifeless hand extends in lifeless air—
Hurled down, as hero, without last softening kiss.
O dearest love, I did not ask for this.

WHO SHALL TELL THE SPARROW?

So blind hath become the human heart that neither the disruption of the city, nor the reduction of the mountain in dust, nor even the cleaving of the earth, can shake off its torpor.

Bahá'u'lláh

<h2 style="text-align:center">I</h2>

She awakens to the ordinary terror of the day,
hand trembling at the saucer's edge,
the tabulated, headlined horrors of the sleeping hours
waiting, folded, complacent,

132

to be consumed with Cheerios and orange juice;
and, fresher still, by radio excitedly magnified
in chilling, urgent precision: framework of the morning.

II

The toast has burnt.
She abandons it uneaten,
swallows vitamins against the lethal level of the smog
and the reading on the Richter scale,
adjusts an ear-ring,
selects the perfect scarf and pin
(only their absence would be noticed) and
clutching the unnecessary leather case
races into the subway's cargo of
psychotic, kind and mediocre men,
in equal fear of all.

III

The man in the lift, with sad and burnt-out eyes, failed saint,
mugger, suicide, or hero maimed by executive compromise,
does not see her. She chooses another car,
welcomes its brisk ascent
to the cool, chrome chaos
of her familiar working day,
its humiliations balanced by a
sense of salaried kinship with the power
of its suave and flannelled men.
She has been invisible for years:
indifferently they accept
her crisp presentation, the knowing poise.
She moves through susurrous corridors
of the polished concubines of corporate avarice,
enters in a bright sprinkle of efficiency,
metallic 'good-mornings' spilling like paperclips
under the brutal neon tubes.
Her glossy smile conceals a scream.

IV

She is numbed by dictation,
wounded by telephones,
submissive to the accomplished sadism of the typewriter.
Decisions are made, stratagems rehearsed,
appointments arranged, but they change nothing.
The sumptuous carpet does not stain though she bleeds
mutilating a notepad during the conference
where her promised recognition aborts
under top-level intrigue.
B.J. beams at his promotion, calls for a round of drinks,
modestly confesses it came as a total surprise.
He surreptitiously pats her with a lasciviousness
made innocent by ritual and absent-mindedness,
delights in her programmed cringe
and does not know she might respond to need.

V

She struggles against migraine to compose a memorandum
in the meaningless marital chitchat of commerce
in which nothing is revealed. It goes badly
for some reason her horoscope does not explain.
She crumples the paper with sudden viciousness,
flees to the cloakroom to blot her streaming eyes
and smooth powder on her hysteria.
Rage has erased the sky;
a grey smudge of disapproval
hangs in the space beyond the skyline.
Like a family quarrel the bruised morning
clatters and chews itself to an unlamented end.

VI

Passing newsboys, palely freckled
avenging angels of the municipality,
shriek accusations of pollution,
infanticide and political corruption.

In the crowded luncheonette,
ordering an impersonal salad,
she tyrannizes the oppressed waitress—
insensitized by bunions and coffee-scalds—
resolves to withhold the tip
and weeps over her hired novel.
Her stomach burns. Repairing her mouth
she curtails the hour to return
to imagined crises amid the litter of her desk
but the Oracle has not written
and the irresolute afternoon
yawns itself away in disappointment.

VII

Her unloving lover whom she does not like
has furtively planned
a concupiscent suburban evening with his wife
and does not call. Gratefully hurt she hurtles home
in feverish fatigue to her selected emptiness
and her Klee prints, the untasted, convenient dinner
and calculated chores. Her hair is set
and stockings drip dolorously in the bathroom.
In conspiratorial concession to insomnia
she pours the earned, luxurious drink
and gathers the comforting loneliness about her.
The door is double-bolted against fears
accustomed as her bathrobe.

VIII

A wailing siren cuts the sun's throat;
it sinks beyond her window in a hazed fug,
acidly orange. She pulls the shade,
tries to remember the sound of crickets
on fragrant summer lawns, but the memory
was lost with the doomed elms of childhood, has
seeped away with all she knew of poetry and music.
The philodendron gasps for breath on the bookshelf,

its leaves layered with a dross of unnamed sorrows
that curl and settle in the corners of the room
like favoured pets.

IX

Flashing and spurting, the evening news comes on:
three thousand dead in an earthquake,
the dollar devalued, the pound skidding,
and hemlines dipping in the Fall.
She succumbs to the fetish for the exalted fatality,
is vicariously victimized,
hears war, murder and other desumed disaster
dispensed with unctuous unconcern
from the lighted, chirping box.
And among the diffuse, anonymous deaths
a cosy local few, personalized with individual addresses,
illustrated by views of draped white forms
and resigned or outraged next-of-kin
gesticulating in bafflement, calamity's celebrities,
their private griefs immortalized on film.

X

Her name is not mentioned
among the enumerated casualties.
With an acceptance blunted by a hidden wish
she assumes she has survived
so cleans her teeth and winds the clock
as is expected of the living.
Beyond the window, the voluble, smitten night,
exhausted by merchandised desire and rented embraces,
is pierced by frightened cries and strange fires.
The heavy air seethes and writhes like a strangling sleeper
in an anxious dream.

O who shall comprehend the anguished darkness?
Who shall tell the sparrow: God has seen?

WE SUFFER IN TRANSLATION

Mount of Olives Village
Israel

Intimidated by the relentless Hebrew sun
that oppresses the dusty garden
the olives have bleached to a silvered insipidity
and the oranges gleam weakly in their dark, glossy roosts.

Flushed with their exertions
the children press near,
wan and wobbling in the unalleviated glare.
I struggle against the urge to reduce them
to gauche trivialized effigies in a nativity pageant.
By now I am a familiar figure,
have been assigned grudgingly a slight substance,
the Canadian who lives here—
someone more plausible than a tourist.
Tell us about Canada! they shriek
in utter disbelief of its existence
and still in faint uncertainty of mine.

And I am precipitated into homesickness
that stubbornly casts up arrogant contrasts
to support my reality,
that aggressively flaunts images of
northness, seasonality, spaciousness,
magnificence, extravagant teeming abundance —
nothing ordinary or moderate.
On my mind's canvas Canada is obdurately autumnal
or gripped intransigently in the hushed or howling
drama of winter's death;
its mountains loom in gargantuan aloofness
dwarfing these dun and arid fibbing hills.

I call as eager witnesses the confident bravura

of colour reproductions of the Group of Seven
whose violent spectrum leaps from the page
in eloquent rainbowed reinforcement of my words
and am reprimanded by the children's reproachful silence.

I have offered too much. Television has
conditioned them to hope for cowboys and Indians.
I squirm under their disappointment
and helplessly watch them dismiss Lismer and the others
with a disapproving shrug. Even Emily Carr
will not be trusted.

Nothing must challenge their pastel parched experience.
You should not tell lies says one prim boy,
his eyes glazing with selfrighteousness.
Israel is better! Our snow is white, our trees are green.
I captitulate with ease before this wrenched credulity.
Smiling, I recant: *Ken, ken! And the oranges, orange!*

They accept the vindication passively.
The small forms glide from my strangeness,
rinsed away by the choking heat and vengeful sunlight.
Behind my eyelids
in profuse explosions
blaze images of the brilliant hoard of Kleinburg
defiantly reclaiming me
in a lush and cooling incarnation.

PART FIVE:

THE CONFUSED MUSE

MEMO FROM THE CENSOR

. . . a poet getting pious is a terrible thing.
Ralph Gustafson
The Penguin Book of Canadian Verse

I've been meaning to speak to you
    about this for some time, White;
I mean this tendency of yours to be found
    scribbling in a notebook every night—
Poems, one might suppose—
A mug's game, as Eliot said, and heaven knows
He is unquestionably right.

> *I concede I seize a pen, sir,*
> *Not every day but now and then, sir.*

A singularly unhealthy activity
    I should think.
Why not, instead, take a wife
    or take to drink—
Do something uncharacteristically
    rash,
Paint the town red, raid the petty cash,
Get yourself thrown in the clink?

> *I'll surely give your plans some thought*
> *But like my chaste and narrow cot.*

And worse (how you do
    compound your crimes!)
So many of the pieces you write
    contain lines
Which have, shall we say, an unfortunate
    religious connotation.
How can one explain this
    embarrassing infatuation
So incompatible with these enlightened times?

> *Would my verse be more effectual*
> *If more cerebral, intellectual?*

141

More grim still, the chilling
    thought
That reading all your tommyrot
So—take no offence—unhairy-chested,
One might justifiably conclude
    you think yourself invested
With—good grief!—belief,
Might one not?

> *What I feel and what I say*
> *Are two parts of a whole, I pray.*

In conclusion, let me remind you,
    my lad,
The spectacle of anyone with
    spiritual delusions is sad,
    but seen in a poet inspires revulsion.
Do try, old chap, to contain
    your compulsion.
It's enough that history may charge
    that your poetry is bad—
But to be thought pious? Egad!

> *I'll write my poems and hope they're true, sir;*
> *But I'll not show my lines to you, sir.*

SPIRITUAL DISORDER OF THE
DOMESTIC KIND

Of all the swains who courted me
One lad I loved the best;
Oft, smiling, sank in pleasure,
His head upon my breast.

Golden were his tousled curls
And blue his pleading eyes.
How well I loved his slender hands
And alabaster thighs.

I would have wed this fairest man
But feared his ardour cool
And younger loves might claim him,
Then I be left a fool.

And so I sent the wight away
(To tell it my heart grieves)
And marked how poorly he was shod,
How tattered were his sleeves.

I prayed the saints heal passion's hurt
For these, we know, forswore it.
I fasted, said a Mass or two,
And felt the better for it.

Another beau came calling
And sweetly did converse.
I noted well his melting song,
Gold gaiters and full purse.

No beauty this, with hoary head
And bulbous, warted nose,
But in his soul I thought might bloom
An undetected rose.

So wed I him and long have lain
Beside my snoring dear.
But Oh! my arms are empty!
And Oh! my breast grows sere!

I bear my lot with dignity
Concealing my heart's thirst

And solaced till my death will be
By thought of him loved first.

I rue the day I cast aside.
That one who might bring shame.
In dreams I kiss my early love,
My dearest what's-his-name.

JUST ADD WATER AND STIR

This is the *perfect* poem,
a veritable horn of plenty.
Note how cunningly it is constructed
as to contain something for every taste:
a distinctively contemporary format,
one

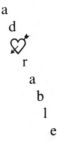

      a

       d

         r

        a

          b

         l

           e

            example of typographical cuteness,
and an obscure but fresh and arresting image
. . . .
to be inserted by the reader,
in the space provided,
to ensure freshness.

You may bet your bottom iambic pentameter
it contains a foreign phrase
(tucked in *currente calamo*)
to enhance the aura of erudition;
a naughty word – – – – (reader's choice);
and a built-in zippy clincher.
The poem is guaranteed to be indistinguishable
from others currently available on the market
and because it is biodegradable
may be consumed in complete comfort
without distressing after-effects
(boredom and nausea excepted).
Intensive research has proven
it cannot linger in the memory
and will not arouse emotion.
The poem is offered in three lengths
and comes hermetically sealed in plastic
for your protection.
You may personalize it
by inventing a title
and ascribing the poem
to the author of your choice.
Be the first in your neighbourhood
to own a new disposable poem.
Easy-to-follow directions are included . . .

    Reader, kindly wake up.
    The poem cannot continue
    with you snoring.

VISIT FROM A PURITAN

*In my view, one of the grave dangers the Bahá'í Faith may
encounter is the effort, conscious or not, of those who have
never had an authentic religious experience, to impose upon
the pristine purity and joyousness of the Cause the deaden-
ing stamp of simpering puritanism, in which the uncour-
ageous, the fake and the spiritually dead take refuge, that
spectre which has appeared at the deathbed of all the great
religions of the past.*

Michael Sears
Letter to the author

My dear, I have hesitated to mention this before,
but after what I can assure you was the
most *loving* consultation
the Committee instructs me to say that we abhor
certain aspects of life referred to in your poems.
It was the cause of some alarm
that one of your verses contained explicit reference
to—was it an arm?—some part of the anatomy.
We disapprove, you see,
of what one might call the baser instincts,
the viler passions,
although we recognize that such references are the fashion.
We who have constituted ourselves
guardians of these affairs
(no salacious innuendo intended)
do not care to have
our delicate sensibilities offended,
nor those of others.
We choose to think
that human sweat—that is to say, perspiration—
does not exist
or if it does that one should not dwell on the fact
that it might st . . .
I mean that it is malodorous.
We believe in the utmost purity of thought
and since you profess to uphold unity

146

we know you will agree with us,
will you not?
No doubt the whole nasty human adventure
will, in future, improve
when we are granted wafting, astral bodies
in which to freely move.
Perhaps we shall exist on eau de cologne,
butterfly wings, rose petals, and whatnot—
pure speculation, of course,
but isn't it a *charming* thought!
We may evolve so as to communicate
by mental telepathy or sonic vibration
which one might hope would lead to elimination—
no vulgarity implied—of the need for poetry.
Think of all those books gathering dust on shelves!
Ah well, enough of that; it is my commission
to advise you that we know you yearn
to have us hold you in the high esteem
in which we hold ourselves
and which, if you acquire humility,
you still might earn.
We think it would augur well
for your development if you were to invite
our instruction in what to
think and feel and write—
not that we for a moment
claim to *know* poetry,
but we know *of* it, a fact which gives us
considerable objectivity.
Poetry, of course, is unquestionably
the product of psychological disturbance
or fear,
and we know that deep down you long to acquire
our degree of poise and happiness, dear.
If we must have poems
let their themes not be expressed too starkly;
we like our verses to be

well tit-willowed, hilled and daled
and somewhat sky-larky,
just as we like our angels to have wings
and their golden tresses curled,
to behave *predictably* as angels;
and we like our heavenly gates well-pearled.
True poets, you know,
in any age,
do not experience exultation,
let alone rage.
Frivolity and humour
have ever been at war with piety,
for the good Lord—as His friends refer to Him—
endorses High-Mindedness and Sobriety.
One of even so obscure a religious persuasion
as yours surely cannot avoid conceding
that among God's many attributes
are those *we* share with Him—
impeccable taste and good breeding.
Poems should be given over to
a rarified cerebral devotion
and not the unseemliness and vulgarity
of emotion.
We prefer, don't you know,
reverence of whisper and tippy-toe;
that is to say, the fluttering wrist
as opposed to the clenched fist.
In your verses we suggest you not refer
to martyrdoms—they're so essentially *physical,*
as it were.
Well, much as I know you'd like me to stay,
my duty done, I must away.
I can see that you've already profited
by this visit—well, you've the Committee to thank—
you've sat there an hour and conceived
a poem so abstruse and pure
the page is blank.

FISH STORY

And pluck till time and times are done
The silver apples of the moon,
The golden apples of the sun.

W. B. Yeats

William Butler Yeats went fishing
And caught a little trout.
A silly thing, I thought in youth,
To write a poem about.

Yeats' fish became a maiden,
Danced him across the glen;
A most unlikely tale, thought I,
Who was but fifteen then.

I caught a trout at twenty.
What use was that to me?
And though it seemed to vent a sigh
I tossed the thing asea.

At thirty and at forty
In each love I looked upon
A fish form mocked me from the depths
Then, glinting, darted on.

Now faint at fevered fifty
I cast an urgent line
And cannot name what I would give
to land a trout all mine

To dance across the valley
And up the dappled hill.
I'd lead her to the orchard
To claim at last my fill,

Feast on gold and silver apples,

A time and times partake,
And know that these, alone of fruits,
My thirst and hunger slake.

I make my home along the stream,
My mourning trout glides by
Nor sees the founderous bone-paved shore
On which I gasp and die.

SETTLING THE SCORE WITH MR OGDEN NASH FOR 'THE SEVEN SPIRITUAL AGES OF MRS MARMADUKE MOORE' AND THEREBY ACHIEVING IF NOT A BETTER VERSE AT LEAST A LONGER TITLE

The Balete and others who speak Setswana
should get along, but they don't wanna.
The Afrikanner and the !Xhosa
are not drawing any !Xclosa.
The French and Germans hate the Dutch
who don't like anybody much.
The British view is quite reprehensible;
they find all others incomprehensible.
Their Empire fell that fatal night
God proved not Anglican nor white.
They don't like each other, them's the grim facts
(It's a matter of 'aitches' and syntax).
Cockneys don't know a spondee from a dactyl
(neither do I, as a matter of factyl).
The Irish idea is even eerier—

'The likes of them? Sure, we're superior!'
No doubt amid the Arctic snow
someone hates the Eskimo.
Pity him, in his most important span,
only the walrus to feel more-important-than.
The Congo Pygmy's deeply loathed
by Africans more fully clothed
so 'spit-in-yer-eye' is the loud retort
(hard for the Pygmy, he's so short).
Canada is a hate-free nation
but just don't mention miscegenation
for whiteman's standards one preserves
by putting Indians on reserves
and placing Blacks in a sorry plight:
'You are equal—I am right!'
Americans discard all such priorities,
democratically mistreating all minorities.
Some think the Vietnamese are nice
though it's rather a case of let-'em-eat-rice.
There are those who have aversion
to anybody speaking Persian;
no doubt one day a foe will sunder them
pulling their carpets out from under them.
Persian calligraphy gives Arabs the giggles,
they much preferring their own strange squiggles.
The Iroquois and Navaho
hate lots of folks they don't even know
while Polynesians (with which little rhymes)
say it's best if you're like Heinz.
Swedes and Finns and other Caucasians
suffer each other and loathe all Asians.
Historically, Brahmans detest the untouchable
which some find rather much-too-muchable.
Those whose script is Sinhalese
quite detest the Japanese
who, in turn, avoid the sainted
Lapplander, though not acquainted.

Samoans feel if you meet a Papuan
it's almost a cinch it'll be your ruin,
while Papuans say if you meet a Samoan
he's bound to hit you, at least for a loan.
Time-honoured tongues are declared now extraneous
to the woe of the Sard and the Alsace-Lorraineous.
The Tlingit dimly view the Haida
and other groups they can't abaida.
Some feel the Negro freedom fighter
could come to dine if he were whiter.
One view it's said there's no appeal from
whites exist for Blacks to steal from.
Yellow hates brown and in addition,
both deplore the beige Mauritian.
Israelis love all people, though—
ask the Arabs, they should know—
but gentile heathens they eschew
which seems the Kosher thing to do
their theory being, if you can buy it,
that God prescribed the Jewish diet,
while Orientals think themselves most pious
because He designed their eyes on the bias.
In Latin climes the noble Quechua
dislike the Spanish you can betchua.
Loving the Russian is no longer vogue,
once hailed as hero, now seen as rogue.
The problem one gathers is largely political,
allegiances being essentially cyclical.
(For a trustworthy guide on whom to vent pique
consult current issues of *Newsweek*
or write a best-seller called, let's say,
Whom to Snub on Five Dollars a Day.)
Mention the British to the Buganda
and in the hospital you may landa.
Cannibals' manners are highly reproachable
(they want to know if you're par-boil-or-poachable).
If asked to dine think twice or then you

may find yourself on tomorrow's menu.
Their customs being so detestable
one can only hope to prove indigestible.
They should concentrate on erudition
and not so much on deglutition.
We race to the planets to spread racial blight—
who'll be the first anti-Venusianite?
Altogether, the world's a mess,
it's rife with tension, it's in distress.
Called into being a strange fate awaits you:
the moment you're born, somebody hates you.
Now, none can impersonate Ogden Nash
but somebody had to settle his hash
(his skill's a fact over which I'm not wrangling;
none left participles more amusingly dangling)
and though the result may be deplorable
it brings us directly (at last!) to the morable
and if morals are something you just can't endure
reflect on the fate of Mrs Marmaduke Moore.

Dare one pay heed to the heavenly call,
become a Bahá'í, and love them all?

PART SIX:

A TWIST OF LEMON

SURMISE

Since Moses was a swarthy Jew
some maintain that God is, too.
I didn't think I'd like a god
who said Shalom and *Rega ahad*
And so I went my merry way;
my life was brief but oh, so gay.
When I died and went to hell
Old Satan smiled and said, *Vell, vell!*

THE GRIM REAPER COUNTERED

A messenger of joy are you
    Who bring last mortal sleep;
Haste not to call, if this be true;
    Will not the good news keep?

Think not my jibes mask fear of you
    Nor yet exemption ask.
Who dies for love a time or two
    Comes practised to the task.

PRUFROCK IN SUBURBIA

About the room the women dash,
and talk of their ills and diaper rash.
Would that the women whom I know
might speak of Michelangelo.

IMPATIENCE

If I aspire to be a saint
Think not that this is due
To predilection for the goal
But shortness of the queue.

SHORTCUT

I try to love my fellowmen,
The Arabs, Jews and others,
But sometimes wish us in the tomb
In sleep to live as brothers.

There tutored by the levelling worms
In silent, chastening vault,
To know ourselves, at last, as one
Nor care who was at fault.

CONSIDER, MR ELIOT . . .

If it is true that naught avails,
No love so strong but that it fails,
All beauty not for long prevails
Nor cure is found for sore hearts' ails
And none is placed beyond Death's reach:
Why, Prufrock, then resist the peach?
The ruthless stalker will not care
Whether, or how, you part your hair.

A SEAT ON THE SUBWAY

O Children of Negligence! Ye are even as the unwary bird . . .

Bahá'u'lláh

I do not remember consenting to this,
the fading hair, the shortened breath,
arthritic twinges; not I
who honoured his father and mother,
who paid attention to his choice of soap, his tie.
This was not the promise of the billboards
and the silver screen;
nothing has prepared me for this ignominy,
I who have never cared for ruins.
Who is this pallid man I shave
whose inaccessible mirrored eyes
look past me toward some lost omniscience?
What do I know of age and who can tell me?
My grandparents were old, of course, but always old,
stirring faintly on the edges of my childhood
like dazed accident-victims whose bandages obscure identity.
Kate Spottswood beguiled me with her legend
but how could I see the merry girl from Sligo
in that grey and aproned woman
kneading dough in timeless rhythm, gesture?

No, I do not approve of this, do not consent;
I should have been consulted. I shall need time
to think about this outrage, muster my arguments.
Let it be understood that I am not without resources;
I have responsibilities, appointments,
and do not like to be nudged into situations.
I am at ease with the familiar.

Will elevators still rise at my command
and the stenographer come giggling at my summons?

Now will she cross authoritative legs,
have eyes only for her notebook and the clock,
cease paying the compliment of challenging my grammar?
When she yawns behind her hand might I not scream?
If I mention an event a decade past will she
look away as though I had uttered an obscenity
or gaze with the vacant, incredulous eyes
of one reading descriptions of museum fossils?

Let me say I am not paranoiac;
I do not go so far as to suggest it is a plot.
But why on sensuous city nights do I pass invisibly, invisibly,
the blade-thin stalking boys in clothes assertively skin-tight,
their flat abdomens, seething thighs,
threatening like an accusation or dismissal?
Can they not see that I am a menace to their women?
Do they believe they invented desire?

Consider: it will grow worse.
I the skilled, manful dangler from subway straps,
consummate juggler of newspaper and leather case,
will watch a girl, a shining, hateful child
rise and yield her seat and call me sir,
her smile the one expended on kittens.
Casually she will turn from my humiliation
and slip through the door, purring with virtue.
She will not know me as the peerless dancer of tangos,
the prosilient dancing youth with invincible limbs—
where has he gone? Is the prostate, then,
the seat of premonition?

And ah, the subway, the subway!
Dare I guess, at last, its destination?
Am I to understand that even I shall die?

NURSERY RHYME

The game is up at last, old chaps,
Come, put away your toys—
The cannon, bombs and ships and maps—
Have done with blood and noise.

Our sons unnumbered you have slain,
Our daughters bowed with weeping,
Is it such fun to wound and maim
You can't see shadows creeping?

Why strut and posture, bluster, bluff,
Now looms the day of reckoning?
Come, children, we have had enough,
Maturity is beckoning.

Humpty-Dumpty needs your care,
Jack Horner's growing weary,
Simon longs to taste your ware,
Jack Spratt now finds lean dreary.

George-Porgie Pudding-and-Pie,
Assisted by some others,
Strafed the children, made them die,
And broke the hearts of mothers.

Margery Daw, King Cole and Mary,
Well see your garden grow,
With mushroom cloud, quite contrary,
And corpses, row by row.

Behold the black sheep down the lane,
And Blue-Boy's rusted horn;
Regard the meadow, mountain, plain,
And fear what's in the corn.

While Chicken-Little's sky still holds,
Bake fast your pat-a-cake;
Goosey Gander's time now folds,
Come, sleepyheads, awake!

The ladybug has flown away,
Her house, her children, burn;
London Bridge fell in a day,
The Rhine has had its turn.

What say the Bells of Bailey now?
What nose the blackbird pluck?
The mouse upon the clock will vow
The Hour has struck and struck.

NOTES

The opening quotation is taken from Shoghi Effendi, *The World Order of Bahá'u'lláh*, p. 77

MARTHA ROOT
See 'In Memoriam', *The Bahá'í World*, vol. VIII, pp. 643–8

A LETTER TO KEITH
Keith 'Nannie' Bean Ransom-Kehler. See 'In Memoriam', *The Bahá'í World*, vol. V, pp. 389–409

LOUIS G. GREGORY
See 'In Memoriam', *The Bahá'í World*, vol. XII, pp. 666–70. For the opening words by 'Abdu'l-Bahá see Elsie Austin, *Above All Barriers*. The italicized words in the poem are adapted from Louis Gregory's pilgrim notes published as *A Heavenly Vista* (see Bibliography)

VISIT TO A VETERAN
Horace Hotchkiss Holley (1887–1960). See 'In Memoriam', *The Bahá'í World*, vol. XIII, pp. 849–58

'ABDU'L-GHAFFÁR OF IṢFAHÁN
See 'Abdu'l-Bahá, *Memorials of the Faithful*, pp. 59–60. cf. Saná'í's lines quoted by Bahá'u'lláh in *The Seven Valleys*, p.9

MASTER CRIMINAL
Eduardo Duarte Vieira, 'first African martyr'. See 'In Memoriam', *The Bahá'í World*,vol. XIV, pp.389–90. The opening words are from Bahá'u'lláh, *Prayers and Meditations by Bahá'u'lláh*, 20

MARION JACK
See 'In Memoriam', *The Bahá'í World*, vol. XII, pp. 674–7. Admirers of George Herbert will recognize his two lines

EAGLE
Louisa (Lua) Moore Getsinger. See 'In Memoriam', *Star of the West*, vol. 7, no. 4, May 1916, pp. 29–30; no.19, March 1917, pp. 193–4.
The introductory quotation is Shoghi Effendi, *God Passes By*, p. 257. Other quotations are taken verbatim from Juliet Thompson's diary. An entry for 5 July alludes to the Master having made public His station in a talk given on 19 June 1912. The events of 13 June are described in an entry for 16 June.

Lua appears to have been the first designated 'Herald of the Covenant', but cf. 'Abdu'l-Bahá in *Star of the West*, vol. 5, no. 14, November 1914, pp. 216–17: 'There are many heralds in this world. . . . *Thank ye God that ye* [the Bahá'ís of the West] *are the heralds of the Kingdom of Abhá, the heralds of the Covenant of the Almighty.*'

THE PURCHASE

'Abdu'l-Bahá states, in *Memorials of the Faithful*, p. 124, that it was the purpose of the authorities to send Bahá'u'lláh to the prison at 'Akká with but a few of His people. 'When Ḥájí Ja'far saw that they had excluded him from the band of exiles, he seized a razor and slashed his throat. The crowds expressed their grief and horror and the authorities then permitted all the believers to leave in company with Bahá'u'lláh—this because of the blessing that came from Ja'far's act of love.' See also Shoghi Effendi, *God Passes By*, p. 180

HOW TO SUCCESSFULLY CONDUCT THE ROBBERY OF A LITTLE OLD LADY

See 'In Memoriam', *The Bahá'í World*, vol. XVI, pp. 534–5. Admirers of William Carlos Williams will recognize the salute to his poem 'Tract'

THE DANCER

See 'In Memoriam', *The Bahá'í World*, vol. XIV, pp. 313–15.
Catherine Huxtable was stricken with a rare form of muscular dystrophy at age 10, was given a life expectancy of 20 years and confined to a wheel-chair. In 1951 she and her future husband, Clifford Huxtable, whom she met at a dance at the University of Toronto, embraced the Bahá'í Faith; in 1955 they were married. They were named Knights of Bahá'u'lláh for their service in pioneering to the Gulf Islands, a remote outpost in the north Pacific Ocean. As the end drew near, determined to pioneer again, they settled on St Helena in the South Atlantic, where Catherine died on 25 October 1967, in her 35th year

FUJITA WITH PILGRIMS

The conversation with which the poem opens was recorded by the author in 1975

A CUP OF TEA

Opening quotation from E. G. Browne, *A Traveller's Narrative*, Introduction, p. 38.
The character and incident are fictitious

MARK TOBEY

See Arthur Lyon Dahl, 'The Fragrance of Spirituality: An Appreciation of the Art of Mark Tobey', *The Bahá'í World*, vol. XVI, pp. 638 ff. Advised of the passing of Mark Tobey on 24 April 1976, The Universal House of Justice cabled to the Bahá'í world community: 'Deeply grieved announce passing distinguished dedicated servant Bahá'u'lláh Mark Tobey. Ever remembered his constant support Bahá'í community, participation activities, devoted services England, Japan, Switzerland, United States, unstinting testimony inspiration Faith as his fame increased . . .'

AND ALL THE ANGELS LAUGHING

Mark Tobey accepted the Bahá'í Faith through Juliet Thompson in New York in 1918. At Dartington Hall, Devonshire, in 1932 Tobey introduced the Faith to Bernard Leach and the South African painter, Reginald Turvey (1882–1968). The three men were lifelong friends.

On 7 May 1979 the Universal House of Justice cabled to the National Spiritual Assembly of the Bahá'ís of the United Kingdom: 'Kindly extend loving sympathy relatives, friends passing distinguished veteran upholder Faith Bahá'u'lláh Bernard Leach. Honours conferred upon him, recognition his world-wide fame craftsman potter, promoter concord East and West, add lustre annals British Bahá'í history and his eager willingness use his renown for service Faith earn eternal gratitude fellow believers . . .'

THE APPOINTMENT

Esther (Nettie) Tobin (1863–1944). See 'In Memoriam', *The Bahá'í World*, vol. X, pp. 543–4. cf. Marzieh (Carpenter) Gail, 'Twenty-Fifth Anniversary of 'Abdu'l-Bahá's Visit to America', *The Bahá'í World*, vol. VII, pp. 213–21; and *Star of the West*, vol. 3, no. 4, May 1912, pp. 5–7

THE PIONEER

Opening quotation is given by Shoghi Effendi in *The Advent of Divine Justice*, p. 63

GRAVEYARDS ARE NOT MY STYLE

See *Star of the West*, vol. 3, no. 12, October 1912, pp. 5–7; vol. 4, no. 11, September 1913, pp. 187–90, 194; vol. 4, no. 13, November 1913, p. 225; vol. 9, no. 6, June 1918, pp. 77–8; vol. 16, no. 1, April 1925, p. 403.

cf. Mírzá Mahmúd-i-Zarqání, diary entry for 16 October 1912: 'I ['Abdu'l-Bahá] would not have gone to Los Angeles had it not been to visit the tomb of Mr Thornton Chase.' The characters are fictitious

SIEGFRIED SCHOPFLOCHER
See 'In Memoriam', *The Bahá'í World*, vol. XII, pp. 664–6

VERDICT OF A HIGHER COURT
Fred Mortensen (1887–1946). See 'In Memoriam', *The Bahá'í World*, vol. XI, pp. 483–6; 'When a Soul Meets the Master', *Star of the West*, vol. 14, no. 12, March 1924, pp. 365–7 (quoted by H.M. Balyuzi in *'Abdu'l-Bahá*, pp. 247–51). The date mentioned in the second paragraph is fictitious.
For Albert Heath Hall see *Star of the West*, vol. 11, no. 19, March 1921, pp. 322–3. For Exhibit A, the Tablet from 'Abdu'l-Bahá, see *Star of the West*, vol. 7, no. 16, December 1916, pp. 167–8

THE COURIER
Shaykh Salmán (Shaykh Khanjar), 'Messenger of the Merciful'. The opening quotation is from *The Hidden Words*, Persian, no. 7. See 'Abdu'l-Bahá, *Memorials of the Faithful*, pp. 13–16; also Adib Taherzadeh, *The Revelation of Bahá'u'lláh*, vols. 1 and 2 *passim*. From 1853 to 1892 Salmán would walk on foot from Persia to 'Iráq, Adrianople, or 'Akká, 'bringing letters, leaving with the Tablets, faithfully delivering each one to him for whom it was intended.' These he would often conceal in his hat for safety. His diet consisted of onions and bread. He was illiterate, and described himself as 'ugly'

EARLY WINE
See May Ellis Bolles Maxwell, 'A Brief Account of Thomas Breakwell', *The Bahá'í World*, vol. VII, p. 707; Marion Hofman on May Maxwell, 'In Memoriam', *The Bahá'í World*, vol. VIII, p. 631; H.M. Balyuzi, *'Abdu'l-Bahá,* pp. 74–80; O.Z. Whitehead, *Some Early Bahá'ís of the West*, pp. 65–72
'Abdu'l-Bahá's eulogy of Thomas Breakwell can be found in *Selections from the Writings of 'Abdu'l-Bahá*, pp. 187–9, a piece of which, '*O Breakwell . . .*', appears in the poem
Breakwell died in Paris on 13 June 1902, in the 29th year of his life

PART TWO: GLIMPSES OF 'ABDU'L-BAHÁ

The opening quotation is from Shoghi Effendi, 'America and the Most Great Peace', *The World Order of Bahá'u'lláh*, p. 81

Juliet Thompson (1873–1956). See 'In Memoriam', *The Bahá'í World*, vol. XXIII, pp. 862–4. cf. 'A glimpse of the Master from the Diary of Juliet Thompson', *World Order*, vol. 6, no. 1, Fall 1971, pp. 47–66, © 1971 by the National Spiritual Assembly of the Bahá'ís of the United States

NEW YORK: 19 APRIL 1912

The first quotation in italic is from 'Abdu'l-Bahá, *The Promulgation of Universal Peace*, vol. 1, p. 30

NEW YORK: 5 DECEMBER 1912

The second quotation in italic is from 'Abdu'l-Bahá, *The Promulgation of Universal Peace*, vol. 2, pp. 464–7

HAIFA: 9 DECEMBER 1956

See 'In Memoriam',*The Bahá'í World*, vol.XIII, p. 862

PART THREE: LINES FROM A PERSIAN NOTEBOOK

DR CORMICK DECIDES

The only Westerner known to have met the Báb, Dr Cormick's account of his personal impressions is cited in Nabíl-i-A'ẓam (Mullá Muḥammad-i-Zarandí), *The Dawn-Breakers*, p. 320n. (USA), and are referred to by Shoghi Effendi in the introduction to that work. cf. H.M. Balyuzi, *The Báb*, pp. 146–7

A CRIMSON RAIN

See Nabíl-i-A'ẓam, *The Dawn Breakers*, chapters 19, 20, 22, and 24; also Shoghi Effendi, *God Passes By*, chapter 3. The characters not mentioned by name in the poem are fictitious

COMMAND PERFORMANCE

Hájí Sulaymán Khán. See Shoghi Effendi, *God Passes By*, pp. 77–8. cf. Qur'án 7: 172 *A-lastu B-Rabbikum? Balá!*

A MOUSE AMONG HAWKS

The characters are fictitious. See Nabíl-i-A'ẓam, *The Dawn-Breakers*, p. 366 (UK), p. 495 (USA)

THE CONJURER

Youthful disciple who died with the Báb on Sunday, 9 July 1850 (28 Sha'bán 1266). See Nabíl-i-A'ẓam, *The Dawn-Breakers*, pp. 222–4 (UK), pp. 306–8 (USA); Shoghi Effendi, *God Passes By*, pp. 49–60; H.M. Balyuzi, *The Báb*, pp. 153–60

THE BLUNDER

Suggested by the incident which occurred while Bahá'u'lláh was being conducted, on foot and in chains, with bare head and bare feet, from Níyávarán to the Síyáh-Chál of Tihrán. See Nabíl-i-A'zam, *The Dawn-Breakers*, p. 445 (UK), pp. 607-8 (USA); Shoghi Effendi, *God Passes by*, p. 71.

Stoning is a traditional symbol of rejection. In Islamic Symbolism, Satan is 'the stoned one'. With shooting stars for stones, the angels repel demons from Paradise. cf. Qur'án 3:31; 15:17,34; 37:7; 65:5

CASE STUDY

Umm-i-Ashraf ('Mother of Ashraf'). See *Gleanings from the Writings of Bahá'u'lláh*, LXIX; Nabíl-i-A'zam, *The Dawn-Breakers*, pp. 410-11 (UK), pp. 562-3 (USA); Shoghi Effendi, *God Passes By*, p. 199; Adib Taherzadeh, *The Revelation of Bahá'u'lláh*, vol. 2, pp. 223-30 *passim*

AT HER LOOKING GLASS

Táhirih (Qurratu'l-'Ayn, 'Solace of the Eyes', 1817/18-1852), outstanding heroine of the Bábí Dispensation; only woman among the Letters of the Living, and the first woman suffrage martyr. See Nabíl-i-A'zam, *The Dawn-Breakers*, pp. 455-9 (UK), pp. 621-9 (USA); Shoghi Effendi, *God Passes By*, pp. 66, 72-7

HOW STILL THE CENTRE

Suggested by the account of the wife of Mahmúd-i-Kalántar of Tihrán, from whose custody Táhirih was taken to her martyrdom. See Nabíl-i-A'zam, *The Dawn-Breakers*, pp. 455-9 (UK), pp. 621-9 (USA)

LULLABY

Suggested by the same incident as 'The Blunder'. The character is fictitious

A DREAM OF FIRE

The characters, including Veronica, are fictitious, with the exception of Qurratu'l-'Ayn and Lt-Col Justin Sheil, British envoy to the court of Persia; Lady Sheil was the author of *Glimpses of Life and Manners in Persia*. See H.M. Balyuzi, *The Báb*, p. 58.

Some will recognize the use of poetic licence in referring to early missionary activity in Persia of the degree suggested by the piece

THE SALT

Áqá Buzurg of Khurásán (Badí', 'Wonderful') was the seventeen-year-old boy who delivered Bahá'u'lláh's Tablet to the Sháh of Persia and was in consequence tortured and killed. For a space of three years Bahá'u'lláh extolled in His writings the heroism of Badí', the 'Pride of Martyrs', characterizing the references made by Him to that sacrifice as *the salt of My Tablets.* See Shoghi Effendi, *God Passes By*, p. 199

RUBÁBIH
The martyrdom of Ḥájí Mírzáy-i-Ḥalabí-Sáz of Yazd in 1903 is recorded in *History of the Martyrs of Yazd* by Ḥájí Muḥammad-Ṭáhir-i-Málmírí. See Adib Taherzadeh, *The Revelation of Bahá'u'lláh*, vol. 2, pp. 357–68

PART FOUR: SONGS AND SONNETS

LINES FROM A BATTLEFIELD
The opening quotation is Bahá'u'lláh, *The Hidden Words*, Persian, no. 26

IN THE SILENT SHRINE AN ANT
The opening quotation is from *Gleanings from the Writings of Bahá'u'lláh*, XLVI

A METROPOLIS OF OWLS
The opening quotation is from George Townshend, 'The Sufferings of Bahá'u'lláh and Their Significance', *The Bahá'í World*, vol. XII, pp. 865 ff. (also vol. XVI, pp. 635 ff.)
Apotropaic – 'Having power to avert evil influence or bad luck.' (*The Concise Oxford Dictionary*)

THE CAPTIVE
Freely adapted from 'Abdu'l-Bahá's account of the life of Mary Magdalene. See H.M. Balyuzi, *'Abdu'l-Bahá*, pp. 319, 324, 348. cf. Juliet Thompson, *I Mary Magdalen*. The opening quotation is from Juliet's diary, entry for 21 June 1912 (*World Order*, vol. 6, no. 1, Fall 1971, p. 65

SONGS OF SEPARATION
The opening quotation is taken from Howard Colby Ives, *Portals to Freedom*, chapter 3

WHO SHALL TELL THE SPARROW?
The poem is introduced by an extract from *Gleanings from the Writings of Bahá'u'lláh*, XVI. See also Psalm 102:7, Matt. 10:29, and Luke 12:6

WE SUFFER IN TRANSLATION
The Group of Seven – Franklin Carmichael, Lawren Harris, A.Y. Jackson, Frank Johnston, Arthur Lismer, J.E.H. MacDonald, and Frederick H. Varley: a band of Canadian artists formed in

1920, whose paintings transcended the colonialism prevalent up to that time in the country's artistic circles, and who provided its first bold and accurate visual statement. In 1926 Johnston resigned and was replaced by A.J. Casson. Tom Thompson was also linked to the group. Many of their works can be found in the McMichael Collection of Canadiana in Kleinburg, Ontario.

Emily Carr – (1871–1945) a Canadian West Coast artist celebrated for her paintings of Indian villages and totems. She was also a gifted writer.

Ken, ken! – 'Yes, yes!'

PART FIVE: THE CONFUSED MUSE

MEMO FROM THE CENSOR

For the purposes of this piece the author feigns misunderstanding of the intention of Mr Gustafson's statement, an impertinence for which he begs that distinguished gentleman's forgiveness.

T.S. Eliot's remark (in 'The Use of Poetry and the Use of Criticism') – 'As things are, and as fundamentally they must always be, poetry is not a career, but a mug's game. No honest poet can ever feel quite sure of the permanent value of what he has written. . .'

FISH STORY

For the purposes of this poem the author has accepted the interpretation which identifies the trout-maiden of Yeats' 'The Song of Wandering Aengus' (1899) as the soul, and the silver and golden apples as the truth in its negative and positive aspects.

SETTLING THE SCORE WITH MR OGDEN NASH . . .

'The Seven Spiritual Ages of Mrs Marmaduke Moore' is a popular poem found in many collections and anthologies

PART SIX: A TWIST OF LEMON

SURMISE

Shalom – a Hebrew greeting, literally 'Peace'; *Rega ahad* – 'Wait a moment'

A SEAT ON THE SUBWAY

The opening quotation is from Bahá'u'lláh, *The Hidden Words*, Persian, no. 75

BIBLIOGRAPHY
– Works cited in the Notes –

'ABDU'L-BAHÁ, *Memorials of the Faithful*, trans. Marzieh Gail: Wilmette, Bahá'í Publishing Trust, 1971
—— *The Promulgation of Universal Peace: Discourses by Abdul Baha During His Visit to the United States in 1912*, 2 vols., Chicago, 1922 and 1925; RP complete in one vol., Wilmette, Bahai Publishing Committee, 1943
—— *Selections from the Writings of 'Abdu'l-Bahá*, comp. Research Dept. of the Universal House of Justice, trans. Committee at the Bahá'í World Centre and Marzieh Gail: Haifa, Bahá'í World Centre, 1978
AUSTIN, ELSIE, *Above All Barriers*, Wilmette, Bahá'í Publishing Trust, 1954
Bahá'í World, The: An International Record, vols. I–XII published periodically after 1925 from New York and Wilmette by the Bahá'í Publishing Trust, subsequent vols. published from Haifa since 1970 by the Universal House of Justice
BAHÁ'U'LLÁH, *Gleanings from the Writings of Bahá'u'lláh*, comp. and trans. Shoghi Effendi: London, Bahá'í Publishing Trust, 1949; Wilmette, Bahá'í Publishing Trust, 3rd edn 1976
—— *The Hidden Words*, trans. Shoghi Effendi with the assistance of some English friends: London, Bahá'í Publishing Trust, 1932, RP 1975; Wilmette, Bahá'í Publishing Trust, 2nd edn 1954
—— *Prayers and Meditations by Bahá'u'lláh*, comp. and trans. Shoghi Effendi: London, Bahá'í Publishing Trust, 2nd edn 1978; Wilmette, Bahá'í Publishing Committee, 1938, RP 1974
—— *The Seven Valleys and the Four Valleys*, trans. Marzieh Gail in consultation with Ali-Kuli Khan: Wilmette, Bahá'í Publishing Trust, 3rd edn 1975
BALYUZI, H.M. *'Abdu'l-Bahá: The Centre of the Covenant of Bahá'u'-lláh*, Oxford, George Ronald, 1971
—— *The Báb: The Herald of the Day of Days*, Oxford, George Ronald, 1973
BROWNE, E.G. *A Traveller's Narrative*, vol. 2: Cambridge University Press, 1891
GREGORY, LOUIS G. *A Heavenly Vista: The Pilgrimage of Louis G. Gregory*, Washington, R.L. Pendleton, 1911
IVES, HOWARD COLBY, *Portals to Freedom*, first published 1937: Oxford, George Ronald, RP 1976

NABÍL-I-AʿZAM (Muḥammad-i-Zarandí), *The Dawn-Breakers: Nabíl's Narrative of the Early Days of the Baháʾí Revelation*, trans. and ed. Shoghi Effendi: London, Baháʾí Publishing Trust, 1953 (abridged); Wilmette, Baháʾí Publishing Trust, 1932, RP 1974

SHOGHI EFFENDI, *The Advent of Divine Justice*, Wilmette, Baháʾí Publishing Trust, 3rd edn 1967

—— *God Passes By*, Wilmette, Baháʾí Publishing Trust, 3rd edn 1975

—— *The World Order of Baháʾuʾlláh: Selected Letters*, Wilmette, Baháʾí Publishing Trust, 3rd edn 1974

Star of the West: The Baháʾí Magazine, published from Chicago and Washington, DC, by official Baháʾí agencies; vols. 1–14 RP in 8 vols., Oxford, George Ronald, 1978

TAHERZADEH, ADIB, *The Revelation of Baháʾuʾlláh: Baghdád 1953–63*, Oxford, George Ronald, 2nd edn 1975

—— *The Revelation of Baháʾuʾlláh: Adrianople 1863–68*, Oxford, George Ronald, 1977

THOMPSON, JULIET, *I, Mary Magdalen*, New York, Delphic Studios, 1940

TRUE, CORINNE, *Notes Taken at Acca*, published under one cover with *Table Talks by Abdul-Baha*, trans. Dr Ameen Ullah Fareed, Chicago, Bahai Publishing Society, 1907

WHITEHEAD, O.Z. *Some Early Baháʾís of the West*, Oxford, George Ronald, 1976

World Order: A Baháʾí Magazine, vol. 6, no. 1, Wilmette, National Spiritual Assembly of the Baháʾís of the United States, Fall 1971